From Seed to Table
Growing, Harvesting, Cooking, and Eating Food

By P.C. Zick with Robert Zick

ACKNOWLEDGMENTS

I want to thank my dear friend Tonja Lee for reading through the first draft and offering her comments and suggestions as someone who wants to start her own vegetable garden. She visited us while I was putting together *From Seed to Table*, and when she left, we gave her three tomato plants to start her small backyard garden. She discovered while reading the book that she could compost in her own backyard. She helped me clarify why my husband and I wrote *From Seed to Table*. I hope others will see gardening can be as difficult and as easy as you make it.

Finally, but certainly never least, I give a bouquet of gratitude to my husband Robert. He's the gardener behind this book and my technical advisor in all things vegetable. This book is a labor of love from both of us with the sincere hope that it will inspire you to start growing anything. Gardening is a part of his soul, so you don't have to go to the lengths he does to create food for your table. Even a tomato plant or a potted herb in the windowsill is a start. Shopping at the farmers' markets in your area is another way to begin. Thank you, Robert, for showing me that even lima beans and brussel sprouts can be appealing when eaten fresh out of the garden.

Patricia (PC) Zick

TABLE OF CONTENTS

INTRODUCTION

"WE GROW most of our own vegetables, and then we can or freeze what we can't eat," I said to a woman at a cocktail party.

"Why would you do that when you can just go to the grocery store and buy them?" she asked.

I didn't know how to respond to the logic in her illogical question. It did make me think. Soon after that conversation, as we weeded, watered, and enjoyed working in the yard on a lovely spring day, I took some pictures to capture why we love gardening so much. I guess the simple answer is the beauty of it all. Of course, that's only one small part, but it's a start.

Gardening is not for everyone. I sometimes waver in my commitment to growing fresh food. It's my husband who has the passion for growing the vegetables. I fluctuate in my passion. I love to watch it grow. Since my husband is now retired, I am mostly happy he has something to occupy his time. I very much enjoy the meals created from the bounty, and I revel in the food preserved for the months of no fresh local produce. But I confess to being overwhelmed by the amount he grows. He promises to downsize, but it's impossible for him to keep that promise. I panic when tomatoes cover all the counter space in the kitchen. And I hate it when his gardening schedule interferes with our life, which happens periodically.

Therefore, I classify us as mid-level gardeners by averaging his obsession and my reluctance at the work needed to support his hobby. Most of the time, it feels as if it's his vocation, just as writing is mine.

Some gardeners do less than we do, and others do much, much more. My nephew, recently divorced, plants a couple of tomato plants in containers on his deck. I applaud his efforts. He does it because of the wonder of growing something that simply tastes so heavenly. I have a friend who grows a garden on more than an acre of land. He spends his life in the warm weather months there. Some grow only flowers.

Our first garden in Pennsylvania was approximately 42' by 15,' which was more than adequate for the two of us. After Robert retired several years ago, we moved from the Pittsburgh area to split our time between homes in the Smoky Mountains and north Florida. He's spent the ensuing years learning about new growing zones and marveling in the concept of year-round gardening.

We grow annual flowers in our front yards and in pots scattered around our decks. Some years even the annuals send out volunteers, particularly at the cabin in the mountains, so we have marigolds, four o'clocks, and dahlias in abundance. Sunflowers line our driveway, and the seeds from those feed the abundance of birds who visit each day. By far, tending the vegetable garden requires the most work and brings a certain satisfaction—once I'm done panicking about the quantities. I've discovered over the past ten years of living with a true gardener that I hate wasting food, so the need to use everything that's edible drives me to preserve as much as possible using the easiest and simplest methods available. Even though, I've done my share of canning, I'm veering away from it into freezing. However, I've included recipes for canning for anyone who is interested.

If you've never smelled freshly tilled soil or rejoiced in the first blossoms on the peas or tasted vegetables minutes after coming from the garden, then perhaps you too would ask, "Why in the world would we ever want to garden?"

My husband and I enjoy eating good food, especially when our hands bring it to our table for consumption. We're not fanatics, but we do prefer tasty and nutritional food. We believe after hundreds, perhaps thousands, of meals we've sampled, the best food comes from fresh—and preferably—local ingredients.

Robert and I married in 2010, but our history goes back to our younger years. We first fell in love when I was seventeen, and he was twenty-two. He came home to live with his parents in our small Michigan town between college and starting his adult life.

I probably always harbored a crush on him from the time he moved to Stockbridge, where I'd been born. He was twelve when his family moved from the Grand Rapids area in 1962. My brother Don and his friend Sid paid a visit to the Zick household when they learned one of the seven children in the family was their age.

"Want to shoot some hoops?" my brother asked when Robert came to the door.

My future husband said yes, and the three boys became friends.

When Robert returned to Stockbridge in 1972, I was a senior in high school. No longer was I simply "Don's little sister."

We dated for a few months, but I was still in high school, and he had opportunities awaiting him in Pittsburgh. He left town in November 1972, relocating to western Pennsylvania. During our short time together, I remember that he grew tomatoes in his parent's backyard. I was impressed because it certainly wasn't something the other boys in our small town were doing. That summer also marked the first time I'd ever heard the word "aphrodisiac." Robert explained to me that ancient cultures referred to the tomato as the "love apple" because of its powerful qualities. The French called it the *pommed'amour*, reinforcing what he'd told me all those years ago. I never forgot him or his dedication to his garden.

When we reconnected thirty-seven years later, I discovered he was still a gardener. I call him a master gardener, not because he took classes from the local extension office and earned a certificate, but because of a lifetime of working the soil to provide food for the table. He began working in a garden with his father near Grand Rapids, Michigan. He first put his hands in the soil as early as four or five. He comes from a family of seven children, so I'm sure the food from the garden went a long way to feeding the growing crew.

We've since moved from Pennsylvania, and my northern-born and bred husband has spent the past five years learning about growing vegetables in quite different climates. We spend our summers at a cabin in the Smoky Mountains in southwestern North Carolina, and our winters in Tallahassee, Florida, located in the eastern part of the Florida Panhandle.

Together, we grow, nurture, harvest, eat, and preserve the food from our yard. When we can't grow it, we try to buy and eat local as much as possible.

There are plenty of books out there to give you the step-by-step instructions for starting a garden. In this book, we share our experience with gardening and preserving vegetables from western Pennsylvania to southwestern North Carolina to north Florida. The recipes and canning guides are ones I've tested in our own kitchen. The reference books I cite are ones I use. I recommend that you invest in some good reference books, particularly when it comes to preserving food. I can only tell you about my experience and what has worked for us.

The blog entries from my website represent our gardening experiences during the time we lived in southwest Pennsylvania, but I've updated to add a few things about gardening in southwest North Carolina and north Florida. As my husband is discovering, gardening in north Florida is a bit different than either North Carolina or Pennsylvania. The garden at our Tallahassee home lies fairly unproductive during the hot summer months but comes alive in the autumn and provides some lovely cole family vegetables—kale, cabbage, broccoli, and cauliflower—and many greens—lettuce, spinach, parsley, and beet greens—all through the winter. It's in Florida where he begins the seedlings that will be transported to North Carolina in early April, so we have an abundant garden at our mountain cabin, which rests about 2,000 feet above sea level, giving it a different perspective than either Pennsylvania—at approximately 1,000 feet above sea level—but especially Florida, which is nearly level with the sea.

A note on zones – In all three places we've had gardens, the zones are on the edge of other zones. At our home near Pittsburgh, it is considered Zone 6a with temperatures going down as low as ten below on some winter nights. The cabin, located near the Tennessee and Georgia borders of North Carolina, is in Zone 7a, with low temperatures ranging from zero to five below degrees Fahrenheit. Our Tallahassee garden is in Zone 8b with the lowest temperatures ranging from fifteen to twenty degrees Fahrenheit. We might get into the teens a night or two, but in the past forty years of living in north Florida, I only remember it dipping down to ten degrees once in 1983. Since 2016, when we began spending the winters in Tallahassee, the lowest temperature dipped to twenty-three degrees Fahrenheit.

No matter where you live, we hope this book will encourage you to start your own garden. If that isn't possible, it might encourage you to seek out local produce at farmers' markets or local roadside stands. You'll find this book filled with mostly vegetarian recipes. We aren't vegetarians, but we don't eat any red meat or pork. Our diet consists of grains, fish, and vegetables. We eat chicken and turkey occasionally.

You won't save money gardening, if you measure the hours it takes to grow and preserve the vegetables. The whole process—*From Seed to Table*—requires time and hard work. However, nothing satisfies us more than spending a morning preparing and canning quarts of our own pasta sauce or salsa once I've resigned myself to the process.

There's symmetry to the work as Robert and I do the tomato shuffle in our functional kitchens. Reminders appear throughout the winter months whenever we eat a butternut squash or savor steamed spinach frozen in the spring or open a jar of zucchini or cucumber relish that goes on top of fish filets before baking. Slow-cooker soups made from our "soup starter mess" warm our bellies and our hearts.

We wish for you happy gardening and healthy eating, and we hope our little book inspires you to take one small step *From Seed to Table*.

.

ALL YEAR ROUND

Organic Gardening

THE DEFINITIONS ON ORGANIC gardening differ. At its most basic level, it means gardening with native plants, using natural fertilizers and pesticides, with the addition of composted materials. I'm not going to label our gardening efforts as organic, even though we might qualify under some of the more loosely interpreted definitions. We plant vegetables that are well suited to the environment where we live. We prepare the soil using organic materials, such as compost and mushroom manure/compost, supplemented with sand to help loosen the clay loam, such as what we had in western Pennsylvania. However, we do use Miracle Gro® on our seedling plants to help them grow faster and stronger, but we do not apply Miracle Gro® on the garden. For pesticides, we use natural concentrates including rotenone—if available—pyrethrins, spinosyn A and D, found in Captain Jack's Deadbug Neem® oil concentrate, and bacillus thuringienis (BT) for general purpose caterpillar control. These natural, organic products are diluted with warm water according to instructions that come with the concentrates. We spray the cole family of plants and beans every two weeks or as needed, based on damage from cabbageworms or bean beetles. We don't pick those vegetables until at least a week after spraying. All of these natural pesticides break down quickly after a couple of days in sunlight. Rains will wash them off, so it should be reapplied after a substantial rainstorm.

Here's a chart to help determine what types of pesticide work well for individual vegetables.

VEGETABLES	PEST	CONTROL
Beans – bush and pole (green, yellow, purple), lima and butter beans	Bean beetles, caterpillars, aphids, white fly, stink bugs, leaf miners	Pyrithins, Neem oil, Captain Jack's Deadbug (spinosyn A & D)
Tomatoes – all kinds and colors	Hornworm, aphids, white fly, stink bugs, fungi (early and late blights, powdery mildew), leaf miners	Pyrithins, Neem oil, spinosyn A & D, except for fungi use copper octanoate concentrate (copper soap), or mancozeb (manganese and flowable zinc concentrate
Peppers – sweet and hot	Stink bugs – white yellow blemishes on pepper	Pyrithins, Neem oil, spinosyn A & D
Cole family – cabbage, broccoli, cauliflower, brussel sprouts, kale, collards, turnips, rutabagas, kohlrabi	Cabbage worm or moth	Pyrithins, Neem oil, spinosyn A & D, or BT
Cucumbers – all sizes	Cucumber beetles, aphids, white fly, fungi on leaves	Same as tomatoes
Squash – summer/winter	Squash bugs	Same as peppers
Spinach	Leaf miners	Same as peppers

To keep deer and other animals from eating our plants, we spray with Liquid Fence – Deer and Rabbit Repellent® to create a barrier around the garden for specific plants. The product is promoted as "eco-friendly," "biodegradable," and "environmentally safe." It won't harm pets, humans, or wild animals, but its smell alone keeps animals away. It's not an awful smell, but it's not exactly pleasant either. I can always tell when my husband has sprayed. He doesn't do it very often because the smell will linger for weeks. However, a good rainstorm will wash away the smell, but the effects linger after a few applications. It works very well. Once he's applied it several times, the animals stay away for a month or two. Applying another couple of applications late in the season should take care of it. There are natural remedies that you can make, but that's just adding one more job to do in an already loaded schedule. The price for Liquid Fence has increased considerably in the past few years, so we suggest making your own using some basic ingredients straight from the kitchen.

Homemade Animal Repellent

Ingredients:
> 1 quart of water
> ½ cup of milk
> 6 eggs
> 2 TBSP of minced garlic
> 3 tsp of cayenne pepper power

Process:
> Bring the water to a boil then throw in the garlic and boil for ten minutes. Add milk, which will curdle immediately. Add cayenne. Boil, while stirring, for five minutes. Cool for fifteen minutes.
>
> Put mixture in blender and blend on high for two minutes. Add the eggs and blend for another three minutes. Strain into an empty jug. Now you have the concentrate. Store it outdoors as long as temperatures are above fifty degrees. If possible, store it uncapped for the first day. You're all set for a couple of months.

When you're ready to use, mix half the mixture into two quarts of water and two ounces of dishwashing liquid in a standard garden sprayer. Spray it on your plants. It will smell but it dissipates after it dries. Only the animals will be repelled.

When we lived in Pennsylvania, mallard ducks from a neighboring farm nested in our yard each spring. They liked to lie in the garden bed, but once Robert sprayed the liquid fence around the garden, the ducks would walk the perimeter of it, never venturing into the new beds of seedlings. But they still liked to roam our yard where they left their calling cards on our patio doorstep.

Eating Local

Robert grows food for our table, and when it overflows the plates, I find a way to preserve the abundance for the months when the garden is at rest. There are times of ebb when the preserved vegetables taste delicious, and the times of flow when we have an overabundance of some vegetables.

I'm not sure we save money because the seeds, manure, sand, mulch, organic fertilizers, and pesticide controls come with a monetary price tag, too. The electricity to can and freeze the vegetables runs up the utility bill. The water to sterilize the equipment may not be in the best interest of conserving that precious resource. However, by eating local food we save in much larger ways, such as the energy needed for long-distance transportation to bring food to us out of season.

I forget about economics when the first vegetables are harvested. What price can be put on the taste of freshly picked spinach lightly steamed and tossed with butter, salt, and pepper? Last year I ran out of our preserved tomato sauce and used the canned variety to make marinara sauce. The tinny flavor and red-water consistency did not make up for the fact I bought that can on sale for seventy-five cents. Give me my sauce made solely with food we grew, from the fresh herbs to onions to peppers to garlic and infused into our crushed yellow and red tomatoes, any day, at any cost. No price can be placed on the value of knowing it's fresh and free of toxic chemicals. Taste alone convinces me that it's all worthwhile.

The U.S. Census Bureau says nearly a quarter of us grow some of our own food. Some of us make an effort to get down to the local farmer's market when they are open during the season. Still far too many of us have no idea where our food comes from and what processes brought it to our home.

Barbara Kingsolver's nonfiction book, *Animal, Vegetable, Miracle*, written with assistance from her daughter and husband, is a memoir for gardeners and farmers and serves as a primer for agricultural history and food basics.

Our garden provides us with sustenance and satisfaction, along with the knowledge that we are filling our bodies with homegrown goodness. *Animal, Vegetable, Miracle* points out another good reason to eat locally as much as possible. The production of food, from the ground to our table, expends four hundred gallons per person per year of oil. That's seventeen percent of our total energy use. Every step along the way to bring us the Jolly Green Giant uses petroleum in some form. If everyone committed to eating just one meal—any meal—per week that comes from locally and organically raised meats and produce, we could reduce our country's oil consumption by 1.1 million barrels—not gallons—of oil per week, according to Kingsolver's husband and co-contributor, Steven L. Hopp.

Now that is something to chew on and swallow.

Composting

I've been composting kitchen waste ever since I had a small rooftop garden in my efficiency apartment in Ann Arbor in 1979. Since then I've composted on a twenty-acre homestead, in an urban backyard, and behind the shed. It's a simple process and begins with finding a container with a sealable lid to keep in the kitchen for the food scraps.

It's not a complicated process, although many folks hesitate to begin because they believe it's difficult. If you simply follow a few basic instructions, you'll be rolling in the black gold of the gardening world as quickly as the tomato plants begin sprouting green fruit.

Not all of your waste from the kitchen makes good compostable material. Avoid the use of meat scraps, fish byproducts, cheese, bones, fats, oils, or grease because they attract wild animals, take a very long time to break down, and can spread harmful bacteria into the soil and infect plants.

Eggshells, coffee grounds, and vegetable matter make the best material to start the process of minting your very own black gold. We buy brown, unbleached, coffee filters, so we throw the grounds and the filter in the compost bin as well.

Once the container is filled with your kitchen scraps, empty it into the compost bin outside and cover with either brown or green organic material. Making the rich topsoil requires a balancing act between green materials and brown materials placed on top of the kitchen scraps. The green things are those still close to the live stage, such as grass clippings, food scraps, and some manures. Don't use the manure from pets or pigs, as it will promote the growth of harmful bacteria. Chicken manure is the best kind if you can find it. The browns have been dead for a while and consist of dry leaves, woody materials, and even shredded paper. We use some of the ashes from our fireplace, too. Layering these elements, with the browns taking up the most space, leads to the decomposition of the materials. Air and water are essential in assisting in this process, but usually there is enough liquid in the compost container and in the air without watering the pile. If you notice the material in the bin looks dry, go ahead and water it.

There are composters you can purchase from shredders to rotating drums to three-stage bins. You can spend from $20 to several hundreds of dollars to make a compost bin. If you live in the extreme north, you may need to invest in the more sophisticated type of equipment to ensure the success of your compost. However, I've composted in Michigan, Florida, Pennsylvania, and North Carolina and managed to do it successfully without expending tons of money.

We use the simplest and cheapest compost bin possible. We bought a plastic garbage can for under $10 and cut off the bottom and drilled holes all over the lid and sides to allow airflow. You can spend a little more on a galvanized garbage can, but it will be more difficult to remove the bottom. Dig a hole about three-inches deep in the soil the diameter of the can and placed the bottom into the ground, filling around the outer sides to make it secure.

Cover the bottom on the inside with the dirt removed to make the hole. Don't pack the dirt but keep it loose and airy. You're now ready to throw kitchen scraps on top. We cover the scraps with leaves from the yard and put the lid back on the garbage can. Every time we put new material from the kitchen into the bin, we stir or stab at the layers with a shovel. It is very important to cover those scraps with the brown material, or you will attract insects, and maybe even wild animals because the scraps will begin to smell as they decompose. The dead material hides the process of decomposing.

In the spring, I fill flowerpots with the healthy rich soil from the bottom of the compost bin to assist grateful petunias, pansies, impatiens, and marigolds. We'll gaze upon the blossoming colors on the patio and take satisfaction in making fertile soil that originated in our kitchen and garden. Our vegetables, herbs, and flowerbed plants will all receive a healthy dose of the soil as well, and then we start the process all over again.

Earthworms are the essential ingredient for turning the scraps into rich dark soil. If I see a worm in the yard, I'll pick it up and carry it to the bin, but mostly the earthworms find it all by themselves. If you don't see any in your pile, buy a small container of earthworms from the local bait shop and let them loose. They eat the organic matter, and quite graciously poop behind nice dirt.

I love the symmetry of composting. It's a way to be a part of the cycle of nature without disturbing or destroying it.

Garden Planning

Two words define our garden planning: We don't. Our garden plans us. It's not necessarily a haphazard affair, but it isn't something we draw out on paper before the spring gardening season begins. Robert goes to the garden and begins preparing the soil. He changes the location for some plants every year. Tomatoes and most plants do better if they aren't grown in the same dirt every year.

When we lived in the north, in the late winter months, he would place clear plastic over one raised bed before the rain and melting snow made it too wet to work. He would plant the first of the onions in this area as soon as the soil was dry enough and the freezes were over. His chosen spot for onions might be the spot where peppers grew in the previous year.

If you're a planner and plotter, then reference books with a chapter on garden planning will benefit you.

Soil Preparation

We don't test our soil. Robert knows instinctively what the dirt needs when he begins working in the garden, and it's a function of the moisture in the ground. When the soil dries out, it's time to start working the beds for the plants ready to go into the garden. In

Pennsylvania and North Carolina, he has begun planting the hardiest plants from mid-March, depending on the weather in any given year.

We've been gardening in the same spot in both Florida and North Carolina for five seasons, so the soil is well conditioned. Robert doesn't need to use the rototiller at this point. It's not good to break up the soil too much. With the soil in good condition, he uses a shovel and pickaxe to turn over and break up the soil.

Before he turns the soil, he'll use a well-rounded organic fertilizer mix of nitrogen, potassium—also known as potash—and phosphorus. It's important to amend the soil with these organics because it's essential to the growth of plants and is usually not in sufficient quantities in most soils. As he's making the beds, he sprinkles the organic fertilizers, dolomitic limestone—every third year or so—greensand, and pulverized phosphate rock. The mix of these organic and inorganic additions forms a dusty layer on top of the bed. He blends it all in with a pickaxe to a depth of approximately eight inches.

Usually every other year, he applies mushroom manure and sand, if the topsoil is a clay loam as in western Pennsylvania. He gauges this application by how "friable" the soil is. He can tell it's friable and ready for the root growth of plants if he clumps it in his palm and the soil falls apart. That means the soil is loose enough without applying the manure or sand. Also, be careful about putting the mushroom manure on seedlings such as peas. Our peas didn't grow through this top dressing one year, and Robert determined the manure may not have composted enough, so it burned the seedlings. If the manure had been worked into the soil deep enough, this would not have been a problem.

Raised Beds

Robert gardened using the raised bed method for several decades. He raked the soil into eight-inch mounds in three- to four-foot wide rows. He formed the raised bed from soil raked into a mound. The space left forms the paths between the raised beds and is an excellent place for mulch application.

The mulch we place on the garden serves as its own compost bin. In Pennsylvania, we used straw from a local farm. We've also used mushroom manure, grass clippings from our lawn, leaves from our trees, compost from the bin, plants that have bolted, remains of vegetables, such as cornhusks, pea pods, or bean ends and strings. This material goes into the valleys between the raised beds to form a path between rows. It makes it quite easy to reach all the plants in the garden from the mulched paths without stepping in the beds.

When we first married, I was cautious about going into Robert's sanctuary because I didn't want to do something wrong or step on anything. After the first year of working with him in the garden, I realized his way of laying out the garden made it extremely friendly for me to go out and pick vegetables. Also, with the heavy layers of mulch between the rows, there was little weeding to do in the garden.

Raised bed gardening provides several benefits over regular garden beds. Because the plants are above the ground, drainage from the beds is excellent. It also helps in aeration of the soil and the plant's roots. It increases the depth of the bed. And my personal favorite, it provides excellent demarcation of the plants and the walking paths.

In North Carolina, our yard had little flat land for him to create a large garden. So, he built wood-framed terraced beds. He's done the same thing in our Florida yard because it works just the same. He plants two or three rows of plants in each box. Those rows are reachable from each side of the box making access extremely easy.

An Equipment List

This list is not exhaustive or required. The items I've listed help us be more efficient in the business of bringing food from the ground to the kitchen.

- **Large container for holding water** – We keep an uncovered garbage can near the garden to collect rainwater. When there's not enough rain, we fill it from the hose. From this supply of water, we fill watering cans for watering our potted plants and spot watering on the garden. Robert likes this water to warm up in the sun but remember to keep the lid on it so mosquitoes don't begin to breed.
- **Reemay® – thin polyester covering sheets** – We use them in early spring and late fall if frost or freezes threaten early plantings and late harvests.
- **Lots of five-gallon buckets with lids** – These hold potting soil, compost, ashes, and other gardening media. It's easy to put mulch or compost in these buckets and transport to the beds or garden.

- **Composting bin and kitchen container.**
- **The usual gardening tools** – shovels, pickaxes, hoes, rakes, gloves, small gardening tools for potted plants.
- **Sheds or storage containers near the garden area** – Our garden is far away from the existing shed on our property, which holds the larger equipment such as the rototiller and basics, such as fertilizer bags, seedling starter trays, and tomato stakes. The garden sits feet away from our patio, and we found ourselves using the patio as a shed rather than a lovely place to sit outdoors during warm weather. We bought a Rubbermaid chest that holds the Reemay® sheets. We finally purchased a tool shed that we put together that faces the garden and holds shovels, buckets and other items that are used daily once the garden is going full force in the spring.

- **Canner,** with canning basket that holds jars
- **Large pot** – at least 12 quarts
- **Pots and pans** of varying sizes from Dutch oven to small saucepan
- **Canning equipment kit** – includes funnel, spacer, magnet stick, and canning jar lifter
- **Blender**
- **Food processor**
- **Large spoon,** either metal or heavy duty plastic for stirring in a large pot
- **Lots of bowls**
- **Freezer bags**

WINTER

THE WINTER season of gardening is a time of planning, considering, and enjoying the bounty of the previous seasons.

When we lived in Pennsylvania, not much happened during the winter, but gardening still occupied our minds. Once the holidays were over, the preparation phase began. The first sign always comes in the mailbox. Catalogues offer hope for a delightful spring. While in Florida in the winter months, Robert plants his winter garden with lots of greens, cabbage, broccoli, and kale. He starts the seedlings of tomatoes and peppers in early January for planting in North Carolina in early April. The hardy plants are started in Florida in early March.

During the winter in north Florida, there is always the chance for frost or a freeze, so we watch the weather closely and keep the Reemay® near to cover the lettuce and spinach, if necessary. It's a time of growth, but it's a tender and tenuous time as well.

My blog entries come from one or two winters in Pennsylvania, so they represent gardening north of the Mason-Dixon line.

From *Living Lightly* blog – December 2012

We're eating our frozen and canned vegetables at every meal, but we also enjoy a few vegetables thriving in the cooler weather. Beets rest in the ground covered with leaves at the start of winter, if we haven't had a major freeze yet.

We pull the beets before the first major cold snap, but we are able to enjoy them several times a week through much of December. They are still delicious, although they aren't quite as sweet as the earlier warm weather harvest. I make pickled beets and freeze some of the crop, but I try to do that earlier in the fall when the beets are sweeter.

During the late summer 2012, a ground hog took a liking to the brussel sprouts and other members of the cole family of plants. Finally, in early October, my husband managed to capture the cabbage-loving rodent in a Havahart® trap. Hopefully, that ground hog is waiting to see his shadow on the banks of the Ohio River ready to make a false prediction as Punxsutawney Phil did in February 2013 [also happened in 2020]. With his departure, the brussel sprouts recovered, and at least once a week, they grace our plates, small, tender, and full of flavor. Most years, we should be able to enjoy them, with reasonable winter temperatures and some snow cover as insulation, until January.

By early winter, the stakes and strings are removed from the past year's garden, and leaves cover the floor of our garden bed. Onion seeds are ordered. We discussed the poor showing of peppers and beans during summer 2012 and considered the options for a better crop in 2013. We know the peas underperformed because of the top addition of mushroom compost when they were just sprouting—too much, too soon. The sweet bell peppers never grew very big before rotting, but the plants were lush with green leaves. Cayenne and jalapeno peppers thrive in our Pennsylvania garden for some reason. Our green, string, pole, and lima beans also produced very little during the summer of 2012, but in the summers of 2010 and 2011 produced well. For 2013, we plan to grow bush lima beans to see if they produce better than the pole variety. For the bell peppers, we will try potassium and phosphorous fertilizer only and eliminate any nitrogen content to lessen leaf growth.

Gardening is a process with lessons learned in every season and "every purpose under the heaven."

Update from North Carolina and Florida gardening: Robert has not quite mastered beet growing in either place. Voles took over the North Carolina garden in the summer of 2019, and he fought their vicious attack on root plants, including beets, carrots, onions, beans, spinach, and parsley. The voles didn't bother the cole family crops or tomatoes and peppers. He's also given up on brussel sprouts. They are easy to find at farm markets and tend to take up a lot of space in the garden. Sweet peppers thrive in both places, but ironically, hot peppers have been difficult to grow in the hotter climates, except ghost peppers took over some areas of the garden and kept the voles away from anything growing near those extremely hot peppers.

From *Living Lightly* blog – January 15, 2013

The seed catalogues appear in the mailbox daily beginning in December. Before Christmas, we ordered seeds for onions, and to minimize shipping costs we also ordered other seeds such as broccoli, brussel sprouts, radishes (both red and the long white variety), lettuce, Swiss chard, parsley, basil, and flowers. After consultation with *Llewellyn's 2013 Moon Sign Book*, my husband had determined the best time to start the onion seeds was in the waning days of 2012.

That meant he started sprouting onion seeds while we were in Florida over Christmas 2012. He buys the cheapest and thinnest single-ply paper towels and places a layer of seeds on one sheet. Then he piles sheet upon sheet until the top of the plastic sealable container is full. He dampens the towels with water and keeps the container in a warm place. He treated his seed sprouting container as if it was a pet, carrying it inside wherever we visited and adding water as necessary to keep the towels damp.

This year he sprouted seven varieties of onions—long-day types—of yellow, white, and red, and short-day type of yellow. He places one variety at a time on the sheets. Then he bundles the seed packages together with a rubber band in the same order as he placed them on the paper towel layer. This way he can keep track of which type is which when he plants. By the time the onions start to break through the ground, it's often obvious which variety it is.

By the time we arrived back in Pennsylvania on the last day of 2012, the seeds had sprouted in their paper towel womb. The thin paper towel helps those tiny little sprouts from sticking to the layers.

During the first week of January, he put the seedlings into four-pack containers filled with regular potting soil with a very small quantity of organic and rock fertilizers. He uses a five-gallon bucket for potting soil (two-thirds filled), throws in a handful of the fertilizers, and blends this into a mixture. Once the packs are filled with dirt, he pokes holes in each section with a pencil. Then he "pokes" the onion seedlings into the soil.

Now the seedlings are growing happily under grow lights in cupboards in our family room. Unfortunately, we don't have a heated greenhouse, but we've found a way to manage. Some people use heating pads, but we've done all right with four-foot florescent grow lights.

February and March 2013

Other seeds were ordered and arrived by late January. Some seeds, such as tomatoes, hot peppers, and butternut squash, he stored from last year's crop. He still ordered some new seeds, even though each year, I tell him to cut back because we grow too much for a family of two. I threaten to set up a roadside stand when the tomatoes overflow the kitchen windows and countertops. That may still happen. My office desk looks out over the front of the house, so as I write from my desk, I can watch for customers very easily.

Planning the garden and watching the seedlings grow, helps us through the darker days of winter. Those tiny plants hold the hopes and anticipation for a spring of fertility and birth of all things green. Robert's goal with his seed sprouting is to maximize the growing season so he starts many types of seedlings on varying schedules.

The winter and spring season of 2012 and 2013 were exactly opposite. Climate change means extremes in weather, and we're seeing it in our seasons. Winter 2012 was mild and March 2012 brought summer-like weather. I'm writing this chapter on March 27, 2013, and the temperature is 31 degrees with snow showers predicted for the rest of the day. In 2012, spinach and onion plants were in the garden by mid-March. This year, Robert can't even find enough sun and warm temperatures to support the seedlings outside so they are still in small pots. Our den is overflowing with plants waiting to be let loose in the soil. Spring began a week ago according to the calendar, but not according to the weather. As gardeners, we're learning to be flexible and adaptive to the conditions, which seem to be changing each year. We hope our plants are able to be as adaptable.

We continue to use the food from our freezer and from the shelves during the still cold days and nights.

SPRING

BY THE end of March in cooler climates, the seedlings are growing; onions and garlic are in the ground; spinach, lettuce, and cole plants await placement once the soil is workable. In Florida, we're enjoying the greens and cole plants as spring begins in March.

During the winter in north Florida, there is always the chance for frost or a freeze, so we watch the weather closely and keep the Reemay® near to cover the lettuce and spinach, if necessary. It's a time of growth, but it's a tender and tenuous time as well.

In Pennsylvania, spring doesn't really begin until April, and that's when the hard work of gardening starts. My blog entries reflect the birth of a new year on the outside as soil is prepared and seedlings yearn to go from artificial light to the real thing.

From *Living Lightly* blog – April 2, 2013

The spring of 2013 is late in coming to western Pennsylvania and other parts of the Midwest and Northeast. Spring sprung on the calendar more than ten days ago, yet the cold temperatures stymied our gardening plans. Seeds sprouted a month ago are now seedlings growing under lights in our family room.

I can tell they are yearning, as we are, for the warmer days and nights of spring, for the sunshine to heat the earth, and for soil large enough to spread their roots.

The onions should be in the ground by now or at the very least, they should be outside getting sunlight for a portion of the day. My husband has been putting them out for brief periods, but the temperatures are still too cold for any type of sustained sun bathing.

The soil for spinach needs preparation. They'll be ready to go into the ground as soon as the weather cooperates. If spinach is started indoors about a month before transplanting into the garden, the harvest will triple or quadruple, and huge succulent and sweet leaves will grow before the plants go to flower in June. Any plants grown indoors need to be slowly exposed to direct sunlight for a few days with minimal mid-day sun during the early spring.

The peas have been most affected by the cold weather of spring 2013. My husband worried for weeks that he wouldn't be able to get the sprouts in the ground in a timely manner. He sprouts seeds on an old cookie sheet and covers them with several layers of damp paper towel. He has one tray all ready to plant, which he intended to do this past weekend. Then we heard the weather report for the first week of April: nighttime temperatures hitting the low to mid-20s. He said he'd put them in the ground even with predictions of high twenty temperatures, but 25 degrees is too low. He sprouted another set this past week because he's fairly certain the ones already sprouted won't last until he can put them in the ground. He put the tray in the basement, hoping to slow down the process.

We're learning to be flexible with the unpredictable weather patterns of recent years. It's not always easy, especially when we're as eager for the warmer temperatures as the plants stretching for light right before our eyes.

From *Living Lightly* blog – May 8, 2012

Last night, we ate spinach picked from our garden. My husband went out an hour before dinner and came back with a load of freshly picked leaves, which he steamed for just a few minutes. If you've never tasted spinach this fresh, then you're missing a tremendous eating experience. I closed my eyes as I ate each bite, savoring its sweetness.

Soon we will have so much spinach, I'll have to blanch it and put away in freezer bags for the winter. It won't taste quite as fresh but it certainly will taste better than anything Popeye managed to inhale from a can to manufacture his strength.

Many folks may not know this, and it might not be polite to mention, but I will. Spinach is a great digestive cleanser. I'm feeling quite refreshed this morning.

From *Living Lightly* blog – May 20, 2012

We froze twelve bags of spinach this morning—each bag contains two servings. Before we started the process, I sought out several sources to be reminded of how to do this correctly so spinach tastes almost fresh when thawed.

Four days ago, my husband picked the spinach. He waited for a dry day and picked late afternoon. The spinach was very dry, and he packed it in a grocery bag. He removed all the air before tying the bag shut. Then we placed it in a second bag and put it in the refrigerator. He did three bags this way. We couldn't get to the next step until this morning, but because the spinach had been put away dry and without air, it was as fresh as when he picked it. It's preferable to freeze immediately after picking; however, if that is impossible (as it was for us this week), this is a good alternative. Keeping it dry is a must. We don't wash the leaves until we're ready to freeze, and Robert doesn't pick spinach until late in the day so all the dew has dried.

We'll probably get another dozen bags before the spinach growing season ends in the next few weeks. However, my husband is concerned because our weather has been very hot here in western Pennsylvania the last few days, and he believes the spinach could bolt and go to seed.

From *Living Lightly* blog – May 29, 2012

We spent Memorial Day weekend trying to get the rest of the plants in the ground. Robert started all the plants from seeds beginning in February. Some of those original seedlings traveled from Key West all the way back to our home near Pittsburgh encased in wet paper towels and held in plastic containers in our luggage. All survived the journey.

I put all the plants we were unable to get into the ground, including tomatoes and zucchini ready to bust out of their pots, on the front lawn for neighbors to take. Our mail delivery woman, Joyce, decided she would take them all. She offered to pay for the plants, but I told her our payment was giving these plants to a good home. It's good to eat local even if the seeds were sprouted in the Florida Keys!

[Note: When the tomatoes started producing in July, I wondered where the small grape tomatoes were from past seasons. Before I had a chance to ask Robert, Joyce came to the house one morning with a bowl filled with those sweet little grape-shaped delicacies. "My husband wanted me to thank you so much for the plants with the grape tomatoes," she said.

No wonder we didn't have any, part of the plants we gave away were small because they were grape tomato plants. It's probably a good idea to label your seedlings so you can have a variety of types of tomatoes.

We froze another sixteen bags of spinach on Saturday, bringing total bags to twenty-eight. That's probably about all I'll freeze this year. Many of the plants have already gone to seed. However, some of the older variety of flat-leafed spinach are resisting our heat and dryness and still putting food on the table. Last night, we had a big pot of steamed spinach. We may have another couple of weeks to enjoy those fresh treats.

Robert created a 25' x 4' spot to plant eleven raspberry plants this month. We have several varieties and five of them may be providing fruit by June next year. The fall bearing varieties will produce this first year planted.

Four more tomato plants went in the garden last week, bringing the total to fourteen plants. Somehow, he found another four plants, which means we'll have eighteen plants, down from twenty-three from the year before.

It's been back-breaking work in the heat, but we're hoping it rains today. The thunder is rumbling outside.

From *Living Lightly* blog – June 7, 2012

The garden is growing at a rapid pace. We only have four more tomato plants to put in the ground, and then it's time to sit back and wait for the bounty. We've frozen forty bags of spinach, and I still have two bags in the refrigerator. Last night, I steamed some to go with fish and rice, and it didn't even make a dent in one of the bags. I'm going to take one of the bags to a friend this morning because I'm not sure we can eat it fast enough.

Last night, we also ate our first cucumbers. The two we picked were crisp and juicy at the same time. I can't wait to make pickles this year. Last year we didn't have enough to do anything so I missed both the dill and chips I put up.

Onions are popping up out of the ground. As soon as I finish using up the store-bought varieties, I'll be heading to the garden and using them, as I need them. They store very nicely in our basement, too. The onions will be wonderful in all the sauces I make with our tomatoes and peppers. Speaking of tomatoes, the leaves are green and healthy and developing blossoms. So is the zucchini, which should be overflowing in the garden any minute.

I have a great zucchini relish recipe we've made two years in a row. I just opened the last jar of it this week. Our favorite way to use it (besides in tuna and potato salad) is to put it on fish before baking.

It's a great time of year for sure, and the best time to take a breather before the work starts up again. Last year when we had twenty-three tomato plants, it was a bit much keeping up with the produce. This year he only put in eighteen, but we'll still be rolling in the red and orange come August.

From *Living Lightly* blog – June 12, 2012

Last night, we managed to eat a meal mostly provided by our garden. A vase graced our table filled with flowers from plants and herbs gone to seed, along with a very few wild irises growing at the edge of the woods in our backyard. Tall purple flowers come from radish leaves gone to seed; long drooping yellow flowers from our oregano plant leftover from last year, and basil leaves peek out from the front of the vase. Beauty graces our home and our plates.

A zucchini greeted me yesterday morning when I did my daily walk around the perimeter of the garden. At eight-inches, this lovely vegetable was the perfect size for grilling. I found one small cucumber to provide a little bit of crispness to our meal.

We picked enough beans for a small serving each. The onions are just popping up out of the ground so I decided some of the sweet "Vidalia" type would be great on the grill. And in the big sink, I soaked the last of the leaves of spinach for this year.

I put the spinach and beans on the stove to steam and then prepared the zucchini and onions for grilling. I did use one sweet red pepper from the grocery, as it will be more than a month before peppers are ready for eating. For a marinade for grilling the vegetables, I used olive oil, balsamic vinegar, lemon juice, tarragon, and thyme. Next, I prepared the salmon for grilling. I used the last of our zucchini relish from last year as a marinade for the fish, and then plopped a few springs of our parsley on top before loosely wrapping in aluminum foil and grilling along with the vegetables for about 20-25 minutes at 400 degrees. After the grilled items cooked for 15 minutes, I turned the burners on the other vegetables. Then I prepared our cute little cucumber – a delicacy at this point in the season. I presented our "almost all homegrown dinner" to my husband as a thank you to all his hard work for growing this bounty. I forgot to mention, for an appetizer, we ate the first peas from the garden. We were probably a little premature, but they are extremely sweet. We managed about ten peas each as a preview to our coming attractions.

The crisper is filling faster than we can eat the vegetables, but we don't have quite enough yet to start preserving, although I think I'll start grating and freezing zucchini in two-cup portions to use in recipes for bread later today. We're getting ready to go out on the boat this afternoon so I wanted to make a picnic lunch. We picked about two cups of green beans this morning, so I made a green bean salad. The garden is really growing fast now despite our lack of rain. However, nature provides and right after I started writing this post, the rain started—our first in two weeks. It gently laps at my windowpane as I type.

Last night, we grilled zucchini, small onions, and potatoes and steamed green beans. Everything but the potatoes came from the garden, but my husband assures me we'll be rolling in spuds very soon. He brought in some yellow squash too, but I didn't have room for that on the grill so we'll have that tonight.

He also brought in two more zucchinis so I better get the zucchini relish recipe out and start thinking about putting up some jars of that. Anyone who gardens even a little bit knows the truth about zucchini. Once it starts putting out those beautiful blossoms, you need to be ready to do something with the bounty. We grill it, sauté it with onions, shred it for bread, and thanks to a recipe I found two years ago in the *Ball Blue Book Guide to Preserving*, I make relish with it.

The tomato plants are outrageously big and green. I'm resting a bit right now because within a month I'll be up to my bangs in toms ripening on the windowsill, waiting to be plopped into my boiling cauldron of herbs and peppers and onions. Soon I'll be eating my favorite lunch of all time: tomato, lettuce, and mayonnaise sandwich. The tallest plants are a variety called potato-leaf tomato—you can tell them apart from the rest by the big leaves that look just like a potato plant. It's a red Brandywine heirloom tomato.

The first tomatoes are beginning the work of turning red on the vine. We're also eating peas—a handful at a time. The crop isn't producing as it did last year.

May 2013

As noted in my blog entries from spring 2012, our peas didn't produce very well last year. Robert discovered too late that he'd put mushroom manure top dressing when he prepared the raised bed for the pea seedlings. The manure is too strong for the emerging little guys to handle. This year the seedlings went into the ground—around the first week of April—without the addition of the mushroom manure. Soon we'll be snapping open pods and eating the green candy straight from our garden.

SUMMER

WHEN SUMMER begins, we rest for a few weeks, watching over the garden's growth as flowers appear and some vegetables begin peeking out from under green leaves. Early summer represents the calm before the storm in the life of a gardener in Pennsylvania and North Carolina. In Florida, the growing season is winding down, and we pull most everything from the garden before heading to the mountains.

At the cabin, my husband prowls the rows of the garden, watching for signs of animals and pests. He waters, if necessary. I begin my preparations in the kitchen, counting jars and lids, combing through the spice and herb cabinet, seeking out recipes, and generally making sure I'm fully ready for the onslaught of vegetables that marks the months of July and August. The quiet ends toward the end of June in the Smokies.

By June in Pennsylvania, as reflected in my blog posts, the spring crop shows itself and lands squarely on the countertops awaiting decisions on whether to eat or freeze.

From *Living Lightly* blog – June 26, 2012

I spent last night in a whirlwind in the kitchen. I decided it was time to use up all the bounty in some way. My husband picked broccoli in the morning because the rabbits have discovered the leaves of the plant and love to munch on them. We had a bag of spinach picked two days earlier waiting for me to do something with them. And the zucchini threatened to overflow the crisper. As I worked on preserving and creating dinner, Robert worked in the garden. After I called him into eat, I heard him enter the house. Yes, I'd cleared out the fridge of the current produce, but I knew I wasn't finished. I heard the rustle of a plastic bag as Robert let the air out of a bag of green beans and then another bag of peas. I haven't gone into the fridge to see what else is there, but rest assured, we'll have another dinner of fresh vegetables tonight. I'm not complaining. As I worked last night in the kitchen, dirtying dishes and floor, I felt a calmness and peacefulness come over me. I describe it as grace that comes from participating in nature's abundant cycle as shredded zucchini flew out of the food processor and into my hair. But enough of my sentimental journey. Here's the work I accomplished last night:

Zucchini – I decided I didn't have enough to do at least 8 half pints of relish. The recipe I use makes 4 half pints, but I double it. I don't can food unless I can fill the canner; otherwise, I'm wasting a lot of energy and water for very little return. So, I made two loaves of zucchini bread instead. Why do all the recipes for zucchini bread call for so much oil and sugar? I usually up the amount of zucchini—it's a very moist vegetable—and add a little bit of skim milk instead of the oil. I've also used applesauce or maple syrup in place of sugar. I always use less sugar in everything I make, and last night I cut back even more by adding dates to the bread; raisins are also a great addition. I froze one loaf, and we'll munch on the other during the next week. I ate a slice for breakfast, and Robert took a slice for his lunch. Yummy, but I still had about six cups of shredded zucchini leftover so I decided to freeze it in two-cup servings, which is the amount I use to make two loaves of bread. I bought a new preserving book yesterday. *The Big Book of Preserving the Harvest* provided instructions for steam blanching the zucchini. I placed two cups of shredded zucchini in my steamer basket that was in a pot with an inch of boiling water. I steamed for two minutes and then placed in ice water for another two minutes. I strained it in the colander and placed in freezer bags. It was a very quick process and probably the best for retaining vitamins, minerals, texture, and color when thawed.

Spinach – Then I ventured into dinner recreating a recipe I used to make twenty years ago. This is always risky because I'm using my memory for the recipe. But of course, I also have a little knowledge about cooking. I decided to make Greek pizza with the spinach. As I put it together, I realized all the vegetables in the pizza came from the garden. That's not been the case so far this summer, so we are making progress. Steamed broccoli provided a side dish.

My memory served me well, if Robert's comment at dinner is any indication. "You can make this pizza for every meal if you want," he said between mouthfuls of the pizza.

From *Living Lightly* blog – July 12, 2012

I've been canning off and on for the past thirty years, and it seems each time I put something up, I learn something new. The other night I canned seven jars of bread and butter pickles using a recipe in Ball's *Blue Book Guide to Preserving*. They didn't specify whether to use white or cider vinegar so I started perusing the beginning pages (*for beginners*, I thought). I read that white vinegar needed to be five percent acidity and not diluted with water. Interesting, but I didn't think relevant. I checked my Heinz cider vinegar's label, and it said *five percent*. Then I grabbed the gallon of cheap white vinegar I bought last week. I think I saved a dollar on the big container. Now why would I try to save on the cheapest yet most useful commodity in the kitchen? I have no idea, except I probably thought there was no difference. This label said, "four percent acidity, diluted with water."

Sometimes it doesn't pay to save a buck. It was my choice which vinegar I used. Cider vinegar can color white vegetables in the canning process, but a lower acidity in the vinegar can run the risk of not preserving as well. So, I decided to use a combo of both vinegars in this recipe. I also added some of our dried cayenne peppers from last year to the mix so there's a little heat with the sweetness of the bread and butter mix. The result? Perfection! Crisp and flavorful bread and butter chips, with a hint of heat. Next—dill pickles!

From *Living Lightly* blog – July 16, 2012

My husband Robert lives and breathes the garden almost the whole year. During the winter, he's planning and drying the seeds from the previous year's bounty, such as he did this year with the potato-leaf tomato seeds. When the first of the beefsteak-size tomatoes began ripening this week, I've never seen him more excited. He agonized when to pick it. He wanted it as ripe as possible on the vine, but he didn't want the pesky and abundant rabbits this year to start nibbling on it. In ancient times, the tomato was a delicacy viewed as the "love fruit" because of its supposed aphrodisiac-qualities. It never made much sense to me, until I saw the excitement in Robert for this one versatile fruit coming into its maturity. True love grows, blossoms, blooms, and spreads here in the garden.

There are differences in the tomato-leaf varieties, either regular or potato leaf. They are very distinctive in the garden. The type of seed used for our plants is Brandywine. The tomatoes are very "beefy" and wonderful to use in sauces. We have a variety of plants in the garden this year, and slowly they are coming into their own. We can't wait to chomp into the three sitting in the windowsill right now. But we still have plenty more. Soon we'll be covered in juice and seeds as we begin preserving all of this bounty. Now I understand why it's an aphrodisiac—I'm in love with this vegetable, and so is Robert. The whole process—from washing the tomatoes to pulling the jars of sauce out of the canner—probably takes four hours. It's not a cost-effective process if only dollars and cents are factored. But there's other considerations. Nutritionally, the minerals and vitamins from the vegetables are outstanding. The taste alone justifies the time.

And then there's the other and perhaps the most important part. Robert and I love working together in our kitchen handling the vegetables we've nurtured. We handle the tomatoes and other vegetables with loving care. I am lost in the texture of the tomato as I squeeze each one. The smell of garlic and onion sautéing in olive oil beats eau de cologne any day. For mere hours, we are suspended and lost in the garden of our creation. The love we pour into our concoctions cannot be calculated by any cost analysis.

As the sauce simmers and boils down, we begin taking the pulp and straining it into juice. Then it's time for our Bloody Mary or Maria (with tequila) or Virgin (without the alcohol) with juice from our garden. Last night we savored our first taste of the sauce on pasta. I wanted the flavors to meld so I let a meal-sized portion rest in the fridge for two days. We both agreed this year's batch is definitely the best – until next year rolls around.

From *Living Lightly* blog – July 18, 2012

It starts innocently enough. The beautiful blossom and then a medium-sized zucchini perfect for quartering and putting on the grill with other vegetables appears one day in the garden. A few more are on the vine the next day. Then on a day such as I had yesterday, I go to the garden and zucchini bats have appeared. That's precisely the reason I self-published my first book thirty years ago. I was living in

Ann Arbor at the time and had a small rooftop garden. I was growing zucchini, tomatoes, and peppers in large containers. Before I knew it, my small efficiency apartment was overcome with the green bats. Everywhere I went that summer, folks were saying they didn't know what to do with their zucchini. So, I wrote recipes, for the *Zucchini Cookbook*. I sold out the 200 I printed by the end of the summer for a dollar each. I still use that cookbook today.

From *Living Lightly* blog – August 9, 2012

We're eating tomatoes with every meal and still the windowsills in our home are filled with the beautiful red bounty of summer. The tomato is one of the most versatile of vegetables because tastes fantastic raw, but it's also a wonder for turning into a myriad of sauces and dishes.

As the counters and windowsills fill with tomatoes, I know it's almost time to pull out the canner and begin making sauce. I'm not going to sugarcoat this process—it's time-consuming and requires two people if you're doing any amount at all of sauce. My husband and I love growing the vegetables, and as hard as it is to do, we love preserving it as well. When I served a sampling of the sauce we'd created the other night, we both sighed in contentment at the flavors provided by food we grew right outside our den door. Besides, if we weren't making our own food, we'd probably just be sitting in front of the television. There's plenty of time for that when the weather turns cold.

From *Living Lightly* blog – August 13, 2012

Two of our herbs have done remarkably well this year. I have basil planted in the ground and in pots and all seem to love to heat and alternating dry and wet conditions. The sage took over this year in the same spot where we'd successfully grown parsley in the past two years, even through our mild winter. However, the parsley has done very little this spring and summer, and I miss it.

We've been drying our sage for burning in the house as a purifier. When I went to find a page for the many wonderful uses of sage, I discovered the burning of it does more than cleanse our spirits and our homes—it also has medicinal properties for sinuses and headaches. Maybe this is why my migraines have finally disappeared this week. We pulled the sage down from the light fixture a few days ago and have been burning it in a large shell all over the house. I'm very impressed.

Basil is one of my favorite herbs. It's easy to grow and works in just about any dish. It is beautiful cut and placed in a vase with water. I cut off the leaves as needed. In the past, it seemed the leaves wilted after a few days. However, this summer I filled a small container with water and cut stems and it lasted for more than a month. It even rooted so now I have another basil plant in a pot outside. I hope to keep that going through the winter. All of my basil plants were headed to seed recently, so I gave them a trim. I ended up with this vase full, plus eight cups of leaves. It's time to make pesto.

From *Living Lightly* blog – August 28, 2012
This past weekend we put up seven quarts of Italian sauce from our tomatoes, peppers, onion, garlic, and basil.

This is our third year for preserving the harvest from our garden. We've developed a rhythm for our time in the kitchen as we make sauce. My husband washes, peels, and cuts up the tomatoes, peppers, and onions. I prepare the garlic and basil. I squeeze the juice and seeds out of the tomatoes after my husband does his thing with them. Sometimes the process bogs down because he pulls out seeds from the very best to use next year.

From *Living Lightly* blog – September 18, 2012
Vegetables are works of art as well as sustenance. Last year, we had an abundance of cayenne peppers so I decided they would become a decoration in the kitchen. I strung them up and hung them in front of a cupboard with some of my favorite dishes. When I need a little zest while cooking, I pull off one of the dried beauties and my artful creation becomes a part of our dinner.

We had some small pumpkins crop up earlier in the summer— we're not sure where they came from, but they're too small to eat. In contrast, while we were on vacation some of our yellow squash turned into yellow bats. I turned both into a centerpiece.

FALL

THE DATE on the calendar signaling the beginning of autumn doesn't mean much to our garden—either when we lived in Pennsylvania or in the mountains—as we're still picking tomatoes daily along with potatoes, cabbage, and beets. I begin finding a myriad of ways to save vegetables for the winter. I've never tried dehydrating tomatoes or other products from the ground, but one year I might give it a go.

I asked my Facebook friends if they knew anything about freezing tomatoes, and I received some interesting suggestions. But after canning dozens of quarts of sauces, I wanted simple. I washed the whole tomatoes and let them dry. Then I placed them on a cookie sheet that I put in the freezer. Once the tomatoes were frozen, I transferred them to gallon-sized Ziploc baggies where they stayed until I needed them for a sauce. They won't be much good for putting raw on a salad, but they make a delicious Italian sauce or salsa. They're a wonderful addition to soups and casseroles, too.

In Pennsylvania, my husband harvested all the onions during the summer. We would store them on a counter in our basement, uncovered. Before the first frost in November, all the potatoes were dug up and placed on another counter in the basement. Don't store onions and potatoes together because both of them release moisture and gases that cause other foods to spoil faster. They need to be stored in cool, dry, and ventilated spaces for best results.

By the beginning of October, the North Carolina garden is finished for the year as we prepare to head south The Florida garden will be

33

started as soon as we arrive near the end of October and it won't take long for us to have greens, kale, and cole plants for our winter for late fall and winter harvests. When we lived in Pennsylvania, we were also closing out the garden and preparing to enjoy the bounty of a productive summer season.

From *Living Lightly* blog – October 11, 2012

The garden looks as if it's been decorated for Halloween, but that's not the case. We're receiving some early frosts here in western Pennsylvania, and the last two nights, my husband has gone out and covered the tomato plants with heavy Reemay® because we're still getting tomatoes.

The tomatoes aren't coming in as fast as they once were so the 2012 canning season is officially over. However, last week I made a fresh batch of sauce with with freshly picked tomatoes. Last night my husband picked another batch, so I probably can make some more in a day or so. I read somewhere about slicing the green tomatoes and rolling them in cornmeal and then freezing them. That way they're all ready to make fried green tomatoes. I haven't tried that yet.

We still have potatoes and beets in the ground ready to eat whenever we want them.

I'm still not sure where summer went, but the pantry and freezer are full of the products from our garden. We're hoping this early cold weather will be gone in a few days—just enough to zap the stink bugs crowding around our doors and windows. As I wandered around the yard this afternoon, I was heartened to see that my flowers stood up to the cold.

From *Living Lightly* blog – October 18, 2012

Raking leaves into piles and then burning them was a tradition from my childhood. When I became an adult, I realized this was one tradition that needed to go. We don't need to send more smoke up into the air. In many townships, municipalities, and regions of the United States, the act of burning leaves is in violation of the law.

The Environmental Protection Agency warns against the burning of leaves because it causes air pollution, health problems, and fire hazards. Sending them to the landfill is no longer an alternative in most communities because of already overburdened dumps. Besides, putting them in plastic trash bags and hauling away organic matter to the landfill makes little or no sense.

It's still a good idea to get most of the leaves up off the grass because they can smother the grass. However, leaving a few on the ground will provide some great fertilizer on the soil as they decompose, especially if chopped with the mower.

We have two acres in our backyard where three old maples made themselves at home decades ago.

Right now, the yard is beginning to look more gold than green as the leaves begin their descent from the limbs. We're waiting now until most of those limbs are bare. When that happens, we plan to mow the grass one last time with our tractor. We'll mow right over the leaves, chopping them into smaller pieces, which we'll blow into long piles. From there it's easy to put the leaves wherever we decide we want them.

First, we rake them around the base of the trees to form a protective layer. Then we load up the wagon several times and haul the piles over to the garden where we place the chopped up leaves. We've never had a problem with mold developing as I've heard some people say, but maybe it's because we use chopped up leaves rather than putting them on whole.

The rest of the leaves we put next to our compost bin and use them throughout the winter as layers between our food scraps. If you prefer, you could even bag them and keep them in the shed to use as needed.

If you don't have a garden or you don't compost, look for gardeners in your neighborhood. Some of them may be eager to haul away your leaves after you've raked them. Remember, the leaves are organic matter, so it just makes good sense to use them accordingly.

RECIPES

TOMATOES

Peeling and Juicing Tomatoes

Blanch the tomatoes in boiling water for 30-40 seconds and remove to ice water for same amount of time. Peel off skin and core. Cut into quarters and squeeze with hands into a sieve if you'd like to save the tomato juice. Otherwise, squeeze into a bowl then cut into smaller pieces. Put in pot with other vegetables. We have a production line going in the kitchen. I'm blanching the tomatoes while my husband skins, cores, removes bad spots, saves seeds for next year and then cuts tomatoes in quarters. I squeeze those tomatoes with my hands and chop into the pot.

Freezing Tomatoes

Wash and core tomatoes. If there are any bad spots, cut those out as well. Dry and place on a cookie sheet and put in freezer. When frozen, place in gallon-size Ziploc bags.

Pasta Sauce from Frozen Tomatoes

Ingredients
    10 frozen whole tomatoes
    2 cloves garlic
    1 chopped onion
    several chopped peppers – I use both sweet and hot peppers
    fresh or dried Italian herbs in any combination – to taste
    salt and pepper

Remove tomatoes from freezer and allow to partially thaw—just enough to be able to chop. I usually leave them out for less than an hour. Rinse under hot water for a few seconds until skins peel off easily. Chop. I find the sauce thickens much better when I add the still very cold and partially frozen tomato pieces to the hot sautéed vegetables.

In the meantime, sauté onions, garlic, peppers (or anything else you'd like to add, such as mushrooms, carrots, or olives), and herbs.

Add tomatoes to the sauté as you chop them.

Bring to boil, then simmer for at least an hour, stirring occasionally. When sauce is reduced enough, it's time to use sauce in your favorite Italian dish.

Zick Italian Sauce for Canning

This recipe makes twelve quarts of sauce so be prepared. The typical canner holds seven quarts so you either need two canners or two canning sessions. Or you can cut recipe in half.

Ingredients
2 or 3 bulbs of garlic, cloves peeled and crushed
5 large onions, chopped
6-8 sweet peppers (any color works), chopped
Hot peppers – optional if you like a little heat
2 cups fresh basil leaves (add any other Italian herb you have), chopped
1 cup of dried Italian herbs
1 cup olive oil
salt and pepper to taste
35-45 tomatoes, skinned, squeezed and chopped

Note: We like heat in our sauce so we put in approximately ten hot peppers, mostly seeded. We started doing this a few years back when we had too many jalapenos and found that we love it this way.

Prepare all the ingredients, except the tomatoes, and put them in the pot and simmer to meld flavors while preparing the tomatoes. The food processor works well for chopping all the herbs and vegetables.

Blanch the tomatoes following directions above. Peel and cut out any bad spots on the tomatoes. Cut each tomato into quarters. Next it is important to attempt to get out as much liquid as possible and seeds, although you'll never get rid of all the seeds, and I don't think it matters. Once you've squeezed liquid into a bowl, cut into smaller pieces Place in a sieve and press down, getting out more liquid. Then place the meat of the tomato that is left into the pot. The sauce then simmers (with frequent stirs) for several hours or until thickened.

When the sauce is at the right consistency, ladle into sterilized, hot canning jars with a tablespoon of lemon juice in the bottom of each quart (about a tsp. for a pint). You can freeze any leftovers at this point or eat! Process the jars in the rolling water bath for fifty minutes. The recipes for canning in this book are for altitudes below 1,000 feet. In the mountains, I add five minutes to all the processing times.

Follow the precise canning procedures for sterilization and timing in the Ball's *Blue Book Guide to Preserving* or some other reference book specific to canning.

Hot and Sassy Salsa

Warning: This salsa is not for mild salsa lovers. However, you can modify this recipe to fit your taste buds. This one won't make you choke, but it might make your nose run and your eyes water, until you get used to the fiery heat.

I use salsa in the traditional way, but I also use it to make Spanish rice by cutting down on the water and adding a ½ cup to a cup of salsa. I also use it in soups. My husband loves it on his eggs, scrambled or over easy. It's also good as a topping for baked potatoes or hash browns.

The amounts listed below made 12 pints canned, 2 pints frozen, and 2 quarts which I put in the refrigerator to use within the week. I don't recommend making a batch this large unless you find yourself as we did with an overabundance of ripened tomatoes. We grow our onions and garlic and use plenty of both. You can't overdue either of these. This recipe is easily halved.

Ingredients

40 tomatoes, approximately 10 lbs.
5 medium onions, chopped
3 heads of garlic, minced (approximately 30 cloves)
1 cup fresh cilantro, chopped
8 sweet peppers, chopped (any and all varieties)
20 hot peppers, chopped (to taste)
½ olive oil
1 cup cider vinegar
¼ cup lime juice
¼ cup cumin
1/8 cup chili powder
3 tsp salt

Prepare the onions, garlic, peppers, and cilantro first and begin sautéing them in the olive oil on low heat while preparing the tomatoes.

Add the rest of the ingredients and allow sauce to simmer while preparing the jars and canner. The longer you allow to simmer, the thicker the sauce.

Canning tip: Always have surplus containers ready. It's difficult to figure out exact amounts. I had to scramble at last minute with this recipe because I thought the batch would only make 10-12 pints.

Refer to a good reference book on canning for the process of preparing jars or check out Ball's helpful website.

Process for 15 minutes in hot water boiling bath. The recipes for canning in this book are for altitudes below 1,000 feet. In the mountains, I add five minutes to all the processing times.

Vegetarian Lasagna

We enjoy this meal in the winter, using our canned tomato sauce and frozen spinach. You can do any variation you'd like, such as adding more vegetables or meat. I've developed this recipe over many years until I've finally found the right formula for having lasagna that is tasty and not soupy when pulled out of the pan.

Ingredients – Gather all ingredients together before layering
  7-8 cups tomato sauce
  Lasagna noodles, raw (doesn't use an entire box, but about 2/3)
  1 lb. mozzarella cheese
  ¾ cup of parmesan cheese
  Filling – mix together the following ingredients
  2 ½ cups cottage cheese (you can use ricotta, but I prefer cottage)
  2 cups chopped and cooked spinach (frozen or fresh; this amount is for spinach cooked)
  2 eggs
  salt, pepper to taste
  dash of nutmeg

Preheat oven to 350 degrees. Using a 13" x 9" x 2", begin layering.

Procedure for lasagna layers

Small layer of sauce on bottom of pan
Raw noodles
½ of filling
1/3 of sauce
½ of mozzarella cheese
Raw noodles
Rest of filling
Another 1/3 of sauce
Rest of mozzarella cheese
Raw noodles
Rest of sauce
Parmesan (or Romano works as well)

Cover and bake 60 minutes. Uncover and bake for additional 10 minutes. Take out of oven and allow to set for 15 minutes before serving. Freezes exceptionally well, and it's even better.

WINTER SQUASH

Butternut Squash

The garden in North Carolina produces this winter squash in such abundance that Robert has taken to only planting a few or allowing volunteers from the previous year to populate the hillside around the raised beds. One year, we had a yield of two hundred of this wonderfully sweet squash. We gave away to food banks and homeless shelters and many friends left our cabin with back seats and trunks loaded down with squash to share. As a result of this bounty, I've developed a few ways to use this versatile vegetable.

One of the most difficult about using butternut squash is getting to the meat beyond the hard skin. But it is this hard, outer layer that makes this a great squash for storing. We've had it last in cool storage (garage or unheated cabin) for almost a year.

Now to preparing for use. We've developed an easy way to get it ready for a recipe and to freeze as well because one squash can make a few different dishes. Robert peels the outer layer with a potato peeler. Some friends of mine, to make the peeling easier, poke holes in it with a fork and place in microwave for five to ten minutes. Once it's peeled, cut in half and removed the pocket of seeds and fibrous material. Then chop into ½ inch pieces. You can freeze it at this point or use it in your favorite recipe. It's also delicious just roasted on its own or added to potatoes or other vegetables. I also use it in soups

Butternut Squash Bisque

Ingredients
    1 TBSP olive oil
    1 TBSP butter
    ½ cup chopped onion
    ¾ cup chopped carrots
    4 cups cubed pieces of butternut squash
    3 cups vegetable stock
    Salt and pepper to taste
    1-2 TBSP sweet curry

Heat oil and butter in large pot. Add onion and sauté until translucent. and simmer for thirty minutes, until carrots and squash are done.

In a food processor or blender, puree until smooth. Return to heat. Some recipes call for heavy cream at this point. It doesn't need it, believe me. I serve it with cheddar biscuits, and it's one of our favorite meals. Heat thoroughly, but do not bring to boil. Serve hot. Or you can freeze.

Butternut Squash Pie

Make it just like a pumpkin pie but cut down on the sugar by ¼ of a cup. It ends up more like a chiffon pie than custard, but it is equally delicious.

Winter Squash Gratin

I made this for Thanksgiving one year and took to a family reunion with four teenagers. I was a bit leery that I'd made a wise choice, but three of the four kids told me they loved this casserole even though they usually hated squash. Give it a try and see if you have similar results. I've made this several times using butternut, blue Hubbard, sunshine, and acorn squashes—sometimes mixed up in the same casserole.

Ingredients

Chop up one medium-sized squash. Place on parchment paper on a cookie sheet and dribble olive oil and maple syrup over the top. Roast in 350-degree oven until done, approximately thirty minutes. Stir every ten minutes or so until tender.

Ingredients

3 TBSP butter
1 onion, chopped
2 cloves garlic, minced
1 tsp brown sugar
½ cup chicken broth
1 cup Swiss cheese, shredded
1 cup extra-sharp Cheddar cheese, shredded
1 cup dry breadcrumbs
1 tsp thyme
1 tsp sage
Salt and pepper to taste
¼ cup Parmesan cheese

Preheat oven 350 degrees and grease a 9 x 13 casserole dish.

Melt the butter in pan and stir in the garlic and onion. Cook until onions are translucent and add squash pieces and brown sugar. Brown the squash on the edges. Do not overcook. Put mixture in dish and cover with chicken broth. Cover and bake 15 minutes.

Combine rest of ingredients, except for the Parmesan. Remove squash from oven and spread cheese mixture over the top. Sprinkle Parmesan on top. Return to oven and bake uncovered for 15 minutes more. Make sure the top is nice and crunchy.

SUMMER SQUASH – YELLOW AND ZUCCHINI

Zucchini Mess or Soup Starter

Chop up zucchini, onions, garlic, peppers, and yellow squash (whatever you have!). When tomatoes come in, you can add chopped tomatoes, too. Add herbs of your choice, fresh and/or dried. I tend toward the Italian variety. For this batch, I used fresh basil, dried oregano, thyme, tarragon and a good Italian dried herb mix. Salt and pepper to taste. Sauté until just tender, but not overcooked. Cool and bag in two-cup portions (or whatever amount you'll use in one recipe). During the winter months, when I want to start an easy soup in the crock pot, I pull out a bag, and I have the "starter" ready to go and just add the other ingredients to make any type of soup you can imagine. I've also used it in chicken and seafood recipes.

Vegetable Soup from Frozen Soup Starter Mess

This soup is a minestrone-style soup cooked in a slow cooker on low for 6 hours. Mix the all of the ingredients together in the slow cooker. Cook for eight hours on low.

Ingredients
Bag of soup starter
2 cups of shredded cabbage
3 medium potatoes, cubed
2 carrots, sliced
1 ¾ cups of tomato sauce
28 oz. chicken, vegetable, or beef broth

Add any of the following during last hour:

1 bag frozen green beans (approximately 1 ½ cups) or 1 cup fresh
1 bag of frozen peas or 1 cup fresh peas
1 bag of frozen corn or 1 cup fresh corn cut off the cob
1 can or cooked cannellini, black, or kidney beans

Use the Soup Starter Mess as the basis for any kind of soup you want to put in the slow cooker. These are some of the ways I've done it. Instead of potatoes, rice works well, too. Just add a cup of brown rice to the crock pot, and it will cook very nicely by the end of eight hours on low.

Walnut Zucchini Bread

Walnuts can easily be left out of this bread. When I'm giving this away as a gift, to be safe, I don't put nuts in it. I've also added raisins or dates or cranberries. One time during blueberry season, I made a blueberry zucchini bread. If you do use blueberries, you can use less oil because the blueberries add even more moisture to the already moist bread.

Ingredients
3 eggs
3 cups flour
1 ¼ cups sugar
1 cup chopped walnuts
1 tsp cinnamon
½ tsp nutmeg
2 cups shredded zucchini, drained
2 tsp vanilla
2 tsp baking soda
¾ tsp baking powder
2/3 cup vegetable oil
1 tsp salt

Preheat oven to 350 degrees. Grease the bottom of two loaf pans. Mix together zucchini, sugar, eggs, oil, and vanilla. Add the rest of the ingredients and stir until blended. Bake at 350 degrees for 50-60 minutes or until brown on top and toothpick inserted comes out clean. Cool on a rack for ten minutes then remove from pans. Freezes well.

Zucchini Cheddar Herb Bread

Ingredients
  1 onion, chopped
  1 TBSP olive oil
  2 ½ cups unbleached white flour
  1 tsp. salt
  1 tsp. baking soda
  1 tsp. baking powder
  1 TBSP parsley, chopped
  ½ dried basil or 1 cup of fresh leaves
  ½ tsp. dried thyme
  ½ cup milk
  3 eggs
  2 cups zucchini, grated and drained
  2 cups, sharp cheddar cheese, grated

Sauté onion in olive oil until tender. Mix onions, dry ingredients, and herbs. Add milk and eggs and mix vigorously until well blended. Fold in zucchini and cheese. The dough will be rather dry. Spread in greased and floured round pan and bake at 375 degrees for approximately 45-50 minutes until firm. Cool slightly and remove from pan.

Yellow Squash Cheese Bake

Ingredients
  1 large onion, thinly sliced
  3 medium zucchini and/or yellow squash, thinly sliced
  2 TBLS olive oil
  2 eggs, beaten,
  ¾ cup plain yogurt
  1 cup Swiss cheese, grated
  Salt and pepper to taste,
  1 TBSP Italian spices
  1 TBSP sharp paprika
  ½ cup breadcrumbs
Sauté onion and squash in olive oil until both are soft. Place in casserole or baking dish. Combine rest of ingredients, except paprika and breadcrumbs. Pour over vegetables. Sprinkle breadcrumbs and paprika over the top. Bake at 350 degrees for twenty minutes or until firm.

CABBAGE

Cole Slaw to Freeze

This is a wonderful way to preserve all that fresh cabbage. Once thawed, add mayonnaise to taste. The flavors are even better in this slaw when thawed than when fresh, even if the cabbage wasn't as crisp.

Ingredients
1 large head of cabbage, shredded
1 large green or sweet red pepper, shredded
3 large carrots, grated
1 large onion, chopped
1 tsp salt
1 ½ cup sugar
1 tsp dried mustard
1 cup white vinegar
½ cup water

Combine all vegetables in a bowl and sprinkle with salt. Let mixture stand for one hour. Bring the rest of the ingredients to a boil and boil for three minutes. Cool. Ladle over vegetables and stir together. Place mixture in freezer bags or containers and place in freezer. We like our slaw with a little bit of mayonnaise so I add about a tablespoon to each two-serving bag when it's unthawed. If you like an all-vinegar slaw, you don't have to do anything except thaw the slaw when you're ready to eat it.

Traditional Cole Slaw

Ingredients
6 cups shredded cabbage – I use shredder on food processor
1 cup shredded carrot
1 TBSP onion (optional)
¾ cup mayonnaise – add more if you like a creamier slaw
¼ cup white wine vinegar or regular vinegar
1 tsp celery seed
¼ cup sugar – I use less because we like it more biting than sweet
Salt and pepper to taste

Place cabbage and carrots (and onion, if used) in large bowl. Mix together the rest of the ingredients in a small bowl and then toss with the vegetables. Chill and enjoy.

Cabbage and Kielbasa

Ingredients
  1 cabbage, cored and cut in quarters
  1 TBSP canola oil
  1 clove garlic, chopped
  1 onion, sliced
  1 green or red pepper, julienned
  1 lb. kielbasa – I use turkey kielbasa
  1 TBSP brown sugar
  1 tsp soy sauce
  1 cup broth or water
  Hot sauce or hot pepper to taste
  Salt and pepper to taste

Sauté onions, garlic, and peppers until translucent. Add cabbage, brown sugar, soy sauce, broth, hot pepper sauce, salt and pepper and cover. Let steam on medium heat for 10-15 minutes, turning cabbage once or twice, until cabbage is cooked. I like to grill the kielbasa first to give it a crispier skin. Cut into 1-inch pieces and add to cabbage pot. Heat thoroughly.

GREEN BEANS

There are times during the summer season when the green beans come in all at once. They can be blanched and frozen, but I've also discovered how versatile the green or pole bean can be beyond the traditional Thanksgiving Day casserole with mushroom soup and fried onion topping. I still make that, but here are some other suggestions. See the section on blanching vegetables for timing on green beans. They are one of those vegetables that does freeze well, but if you use the beans you blanched and froze in any of these recipes, you will still need to cook them for a few minutes in the microwave before using in any of these dishes. I've found even the baked casseroles won't cook them further before using.

Patricia's Marinated Green Bean Salad

Ingredients

4 cups green beans, steamed for about 7 minutes
1 can black olives, chopped
1 can garbanzo beans
1/4 lb. Swiss cheese, cut into small chunks
1 small onion, chopped
Fresh or dried dill or other herbs of your choice to taste
½ cup chopped parsley
1 red pepper, chopped (you can use green or banana peppers)
1 TBSP balsamic vinegar
2 TBSP olive oil
juice from one lemon

Mix together all the vegetables and herbs. Add salt and pepper to taste. Whisk together the rest of the ingredients and pour over the vegetables and herbs. Chill before serving. This salad is even better on the second and third days.

Robert's Four or Five Been Casserole

Use any combination of beans with the green beans. It could be a ten-bean salad if you'd like and can find that many beans. Here's how we usually make it.

Ingredients

2 cups cooked green beans
1 can black beans
1 can dark red kidney beans
1 can garbanzo beans
1 can white beans
1 small onion, chopped
½ cup chopped parsley
1 tsp thyme or tarragon
½ tsp dried fennel
1 TBSP balsamic vinegar
2 TBSP olive oil
Juice from 1 lemon
1 clove of garlic, crushed
1 tsp soy sauce

Combine all the beans—using as many combinations as you'd like—onions, and parsley. Mix the rest of the ingredients in a small bowl, then pour over bean mixture and mix thoroughly. Chill. This salad lasts for days and gets better with each serving.

Shrimp, Green Beans, Squash, and Coconut Milk Stew

A Filipino dish (*Ginataang Kalabasa at Sitaw*) suggested by our neighbor to whom we often give butternut squash. It is soupy and best eaten over rice.

Ingredients

1 TBSP canola oil
1 small onion, thinly sliced
3 cloves of garlic, minced
Hot sauce or hot pepper, to taste
1 TBSP fish sauce
2 cups coconut milk
2 cups cubed pieces of butternut squash
2 cups green beans, cut into 3-inch pieces
½ lb. large shrimp
Salt to taste

Heat oil in large skillet. Add onions and garlic and sauté for a few minutes. Add fish sauce and cook for 1-2 minutes. Pour in coconut milk and hot pepper. Bring to a simmer and cook 5-6 minutes until slightly reduced. Add squash and beans and cook for 10-15 minutes until both vegetables are done. Beans should be tender but still crisp. Add shrimp and cook until shrimp turns pink. Season with salt and serve over rice.

Tuna Noodle Casserole

I know this is an old-style recipe. For me, it represents comfort food because my mom often prepared it. I have modified it over the years, so it's more of a vegetable tuna casserole. I use any combination of vegetables—just depends on what I have on hand.

Ingredients
6 oz. egg noodles (half a bag)
1 onion, chopped
½ green, red, yellow, or orange sweet pepper, chopped
1 cup green beans, cooked
½ cup peas (frozen are fine)
½ cup corn (again, frozen works well)
1 can cream of mushroom soup
½ can of milk (using soup can)
3/4 cup cheddar or mozzarella cheese
2 cans of tuna, drained
¼ cup parmesan cheese
¼ Panko or breadcrumbs
1 tsp paprika – Hungarian sharp gives a little spice

Cook the egg noodles in boiling water for 8 minutes (less than package directions - makes a creamier casserole). Preheat oven to 350 degrees. Prepare the rest of the ingredients. Drain noodles and put in a large bowl. Add all the ingredients except parmesan, paprika, and Panko. Mix those three ingredients and set aside. Place in a casserole dish, cover, and bake for 35 minutes. Remove cover and sprinkle the parmesan mixture over the top. Bake an additional 15 minutes, uncovered. Allow to sit for a few minutes before delving into a comforting dish.

Pad Thai a la Patricia

Ingredients

> 6 oz. uncooked rice noodles (makes 3 cups cooked)
> 5 TBSP soy sauce
> 2 TBSP peanut butter
> 1 TBSP brown sugar
> 3 TBSP peanut oil
> 3 eggs, beaten
> 1 onion, chopped
> 1 cup green beans, cooked and cut into 1-inch lengths
> 3 garlic cloves, crushed
> Hot pepper sauce or crushed hot peppers to taste
> 1 lb. extra firm tofu, cubed
> 1/3 cup cider vinegar
> 1 ½ cup dry roasted peanuts
> 1 lime, cut into wedges

Cook noodles three minutes in boiling water. Drain and rinse in cold water. Drain thoroughly and refrigerate. Combine soy sauce, peanut butter, and sugar in a small bowl and mix until well combined. Set aside. Heat 1 TBSP oil in either a large skillet or wok and add beaten eggs. Cook until eggs are dry. Remove from pan to bowl and set aside.

Heat the pan again. Add rest of oil and when hot, add onions, beans, garlic and pepper. Stir fry for a minute then add tofu and stir fry for a few minutes. Add cooked noodles and separate with a fork to mix with rest of ingredients. Continue to stir fry for five more minutes. Add the peanut butter mixture and vinegar. Stir into the rest and cook several more minutes. Stir in cooked egg. Serve topped with peanuts and lime wedges.

PICKLING

Bread and Butter Pickle Chips

Note: If zucchini has overwhelmed you, you can also add slices to this recipe, just adjust cucumber amount below.

This recipe makes approximately 7 or 8 pints. Any leftover can be put in a jar and refrigerated and used within the week. I've also frozen them in freezer containers. It's sometimes difficult to gauge exactly how many cucumbers to how many jars, so I always have more jars than I think I'll need all sterilized and ready to use. Any way you store it—refrigerator, canned, or frozen—use sterilized containers.

Ingredients
18-20 small cucumbers or pickling cucumbers, sliced
5 medium onions, sliced
2 whole cloves of garlic
5 dried cayenne peppers (or less if you don't like spicy)
½ cup canning salt
2 cups sugar
2 Tbsp. mustard seed
2 tsp. turmeric
2 tsp. celery seed
1 tsp. ginger
1 tsp. peppercorns
3 cups vinegar (best to use white with five percent acidity and not diluted with water)
Lime for canning pickles – 1/8 tsp per jar

Place cucumbers, onions, garlic and peppers in large pot or bowl and mix in canning salt. Cover with ice cubes and let set for three hours. Drain and rinse. Then prepare the liquid.

Bring vinegar, sugar, and spices to boil. Add vegetables and bring to a boil again. Add lime to the bottom of each jar to be canned. Pack in hot sterilized jars and process for ten minutes.

The recipes for canning in this book are for altitudes below 1,000 feet. In the mountains, I add five minutes to all the processing time.

Kosher Dill Pickles

We tried brining pickles one year, which means we put cucumbers in a crock, covered with water and vinegar for three weeks. The same year, we made just regular kosher dill pickles. The result in taste and texture was nearly the same, so we don't do the brined version anymore. It's more of a commitment for little benefit in our experience.

This recipe makes approximately four quarts or seven-eight pints. Again, I follow the same advice from earlier. Prepare more jars than recipe says so you're prepared when you start the process of putting into jars. It's disruptive to have to stop the process to sterilize more if needed. If you don't use them all, there's nothing to lose.

Ingredients
40 cucumbers – smaller ones can be left whole; larger variety either halve or quarter
½ cup canning salt
½ cup sugar
1 quart white vinegar (five percent acidity)
1 quart water
3 TBLS mixed pickling spices
fresh dill – one head per jar
1 bay leaf per jar
2 cayenne peppers per jar
1 clove garlic per jar
½ tsp mustard seed per jar
Lime for canning

Remove all blossom stems from cucumbers. Wash and drain. Combine salt, vinegar, sugar, and water in a large pot. Tie pickling spices in spice bag or cheesecloth and add to pot; simmer fifteen minutes.

Add 1/8 tsp of lime to the bottom of each jar. Pack cucumbers in hot, sterilized jars, leaving ¼ inch head space. Place dill, bay leave, peppers, garlic, and mustard seed in each jar. Ladle hot liquid over cucumbers leaving ¼ headspace. Make sure to insert sterilized knife into jars to release any air bubbles. After placing lid and bands on each jar, place in boiling-water canner. Process twenty minutes. The recipes

---

for canning in this book are for altitudes below 1,000 feet. In the mountains, I add five minutes to all the processing time.

Pickled Beets

When it's time to begin pulling up all the beets in the ground, I pickle a batch. Pickled beets are great on an antipasto platter or in salads.

Ingredients
6-7 medium beets, red and/or yellow
3 medium onions, sliced
1 ½ cups sugar
3 sticks cinnamon, broken into pieces
1 TBLS mustard seed
1 tsp allspice
1 tsp whole cloves
1 tsp salt
2 ½ cups cider vinegar
1 ½ cups water

Makes four or five pints. Wash beets but leave approximately two inches of stem and tap roots. Place beets in saucepan and cover with water. Bring to a boil and gently boil for approximately fifty minutes or until tender. The length of time depends upon the size and age of the beets. Combine remaining ingredients in another saucepan and bring to a boil. Simmer for five minutes. Once beets are done, remove from water and cool for a few minutes. The skin should peel off very easily. Cut off stem and root ends. Slice the beets in ¼ inch slices. Place in hot, sterilized jars and cover with liquid and spices, leaving ¼ inch head space in each jar. Remove any air bubbles with sterilized knife. After putting on lids and bands, process in boiling hot water bath for 30 minutes. The recipes for canning in this book are for altitudes below 1,000 feet. In the mountains, I add five minutes to all the processing time.

Pickled Jalapeno Peppers

This is a great way to use excess jalapeno peppers. You can process the peppers or place the sliced peppers in vinegar and keep in refrigerator for a few months. We do it both ways, always using the refrigerator peppers first. The pickled jalapeno peppers are a great addition to any dish you want to spice up. I put them in soups, cornbread, and casseroles. The pickling process takes away some of the heat, but these are still hot.

Ingredients
20-30 jalapeno peppers
2 cups white vinegar
2 cups water
½ tsp pickling spices
Garlic cloves –two or three in each jar

Cut stems off peppers and slice. Pack into four or five hot, sterilized jars. Combine vinegar and water and heat to a simmer, but do not boil. Pour hot liquid over peppers, leaving ½ inch head space. Add spices and garlic to each jar. Cover each jar with lids and bands. Process in boiling hot water bath for 10 minutes. The recipes for canning in this book are for altitudes below 1,000 feet. In the mountains, I add five minutes to all the processing time.

Zucchini Relish ala Zick

Ingredients
6 large zucchini
3 medium onions
1 red pepper
1 green pepper
1 yellow pepper
4 cloves of garlic
3 crushed cayenne peppers (optional)
4 TBSP salt
2 cups of cider vinegar
2 cups sugar
4 tsp celery salt
2 tsp mustard seed

Chop all the vegetables in a food processor. Place in a large bowl and sprinkle salt on top. Cover with water and let sit for two hours.

Bring the rest of the ingredients to a boil at the end of the two hours. Rinse and drain vegetables and add to the boiling liquid. Simmer ten minutes. Place in six hot, sterilized canning jars.

Process in boiling water bath for ten minutes. The recipes for canning in this book are for altitudes below 1,000 feet. In the mountains, I add five minutes to all the processing time.

We use the relish in potato and tuna salads, but it also makes a wonderful marinade for seafood.

PIZZA FROM THE GARDEN

Greek Pizza

Years ago, when I lived in Ann Arbor, there was an authentic Greek restaurant and they served a "Greek pizza." It was my favorite dish on the menu, and when they closed their doors, I complained about not ever having that pizza again. Using my memory and cooking knowledge, I've managed to come pretty close to what that restaurant served.

Ingredients
Phyllo (or filo) dough – use half a box
2 cups of cooked spinach, drained until fairly dry
1 onion, chopped
2 cloves of garlic, crushed
1 cup fresh basil leaves
¼ pound feta cheese, crumbled
1 cup cottage cheese
1 ½ cups of mozzarella cheese, grated
2 TBSP butter, melted
Spray oil (olive or canola)

Preheat oven to 350 degrees. Sauté the onion, garlic, and basil in olive oil. Prepare the phyllo dough, following the instructions on the box. Layer half the sheets of dough on a cookie sheet, spraying each layer with oil. Mix together spinach, feta, and cottage cheese. Layer the ingredients: sauté mix, spinach mix, and top with mozzarella cheese. Layer the remaining sheets of dough on top, spraying each layer. Brush the top sheets with melted butter. Bake 20-30 minutes, depending on your oven. The dough should be a golden color.

Grilled Pizza

This recipe is one I've been perfecting over the past several years, and it's best made with the freshest of tomatoes from the garden. Pizza is personal. I'm sharing my personal recipe, but you may find other toppings you like better.

Just like with pie, it all starts with the crust. You can buy pizza dough, but this recipe is pretty basic and easy to make.

Pizza dough

Ingredients

  1 pkg. dry yeast
  1 cup warm water
  1 tsp brown sugar
  1 tsp salt
  2 ½ cups flour
  Olive oil

Beat yeast, sugar, and water until well blended. Let rest for a few minutes. Add salt and flour and mix until dough forms. Knead on floured board until smooth (three-five minutes). Place in a warm bowl coated with olive oil. Cover with damp towel and leave in a warm spot. Allow to rise until dough doubles (approximately an hour). Punch down dough and roll into oblong roll on floured board. (I usually cut dough in half and place one portion in a freezer bag and freeze). Cut into ten to twelve (full dough recipe) or five to six pieces and roll each into a ball.

Roll out each ball into a thin circle, approximately six inches in diameter and place on cookie coated with olive oil. The smaller the individual pizzas, the easier it will be to put them on the grill. Grill at 400 degrees Fahrenheit on side with oil for two minutes or until a crust forms on the one side.

The trickiest part of the whole process is making sure the crusts don't burn on the grill. You know your grill best. I've learned to do this by trial and error and mostly by hovering near the grill and watching.

After one side is grilled, make sure cookie sheet is still coated with olive oil and place crusts back on the cookie sheet with grilled side up. You are now ready to put the ingredients on top of the grilled side.

Pizza toppings

(For six pizzas – double if using full recipe of dough)
3-4 medium tomatoes, thinly sliced
2-3 cloves of garlic, minced
½ cup fresh basil, chopped
8 oz. feta cheese, crumbled
1 sweet or hot banana pepper, seeded and thinly sliced
8 oz. mozzarella cheese
Parmesan, salt, and pepper to taste

Place sliced tomatoes on the grilled side of crust. Sprinkle minced garlic evenly on top of tomatoes to taste. Salt and pepper the tomatoes to taste. Sprinkle basil and feta over tomatoes. Put on peppers. Finish with the mozzarella cheese. You're now ready to put back on the hot grill.

You must be very careful at this point so you don't burn the bottom of the crusts. Again, I've had to learn from practice. For my gas grill (which is very old), this method works the best. I put the pizzas on the hot grill and shut the cover leaving burners on high. After 2-3 minutes (without opening the lid), I turn off the grill and let the pizzas sit while the grill cools down. After 20 minutes, the cheese is melted and the crusts are not burned. Sometimes I put the pizzas on the cookie sheet and place under the broiler for one minute to ensure a bubbly cheesy top. Sprinkle the finished product with parmesan cheese

Regular Pizza with Thin Crust

Here's the pizza I make most often during the winter months with our canned sauce or sauce I've made from the frozen tomatoes. I use a pizza stone and make a thin crust. Your choice on ingredients.

Thin pizza crust (makes 2 crusts—I usually freeze one)
Ingredients
¾ cup lukewarm water
1 pkg active dry yeast
1 tsp sugar
2 cups all-purpose flour (I always use unbleached)
¾ tsp salt
1 tsp olive oil

Pour water into medium bowl, add sugar and sprinkle yeast on top. Stir with a fork and let rest for a few minutes. Add flour and salt. Mix together until able to put out on board and knead until smooth and elastic. Add flour a TBSP at a time if too sticky. Place 1 tsp oil in a bowl and put dough in bowl swishing it around to cover with oil. Cover and let rise for 30 minutes.

Preheat oven to 400 degrees and place pizza stone in oven. After dough has risen, cut in two. Freeze one or put aside while preparing the first one. Roll out on parchment paper, resting when dough shrinks back. Continue rolling until dough the correct size. Place parchment paper and crust on heated pizza stone and bake for 2 minutes to just give the crust a little hardness. Pull crust and parchment paper and sprinkle with parmesan cheese. Cover with sauce—be careful to just coat the crust or it will overflow. Add toppings of choice and cover with mozzarella cheese. Return to pizza stone and bake for 10 minutes or until cheese is just turning brown.

MISCELLANEOUS THINGS

Pesto – Basil or Parsley

Parsley in pesto works as well as basil. They could even be combined. Parsley pesto makes a good dressing for baked fish or chicken breasts as well. Also, I use walnuts in my pesto rather than expensive pine nuts. I can't tell the difference except in my wallet. You can also use some spinach leaves if you're short on basil or parsley. This recipe makes one batch and can be kept in the refrigerator for up to a week.

Ingredients
2 cups fresh basil or parsley, stems trimmed
3 cloves of garlic
½ cup walnuts
½ cup parmesan cheese
½ cup olive oil
Salt pepper to taste

Place basil or parsley and walnuts in food processor. Pulse several times. Add garlic, cheese, and salt and pepper and pulse several more times. Scrape down sides with spatula. Using shoot, slowly pour in olive oil while processing on low.

Patricia's Pesto – A Large Batch for Freezing

Ingredients
    8 cups packed fresh basil leaves
    4-6 cloves of garlic
    3/4 cup pine nuts or walnuts
    1 cup extra-virgin olive oil
    salt and pepper to taste

Combine basil, garlic, and pine nuts or walnuts in a food processor (you will probably need to do this in batches) and pulse until coarsely chopped. Add the olive oil and process until mixed in and smooth. (If you want to use immediately add 1 1/2 cups of cheese at this point. Do not add cheese if freezing. Add the Parmesan cheese after thawing and before using.

Fill ice cube trays with the mixture. This batch took about a tray and a half (making approximately 24 cubes). Freeze the cubes and then place in a zip lock bag. Whenever I want to use pesto on pasta or in a sauce, I pull out a cube or two or three, add some Parmesan cheese and it's good to go. Use within six months.

Blanching and Freezing Spinach

Note: the blanching steps may be followed for most vegetables with variation in the time the vegetable is in the boiling water. The recipe below preserves as much of the vitamins and taste as possible.

Wash the leaves – Put the leaves in a sink of cold water and carefully wash off all dirt and grass. Put in colander to drain.

Chop the leaves – I didn't do this last year, and I was sorry. While the spinach tasted great, it was a bit stringy. I chopped them into about 1-inch squares.

Blanch – Bring a big pot of water to boil and place one colander full of leaves into the water for two minutes.

Ice water bath – Submerge in ice water for another two minutes. Place in colander in a large bowl or pot and let drain for a few minutes.

Put into freezer bag that is labeled and dated.

One colander full equals two servings and fits perfectly into a freezer sandwich bag. It's fine if some water is in the bag – it's probably better for the spinach.

Blanching Vegetables

Blanching is the process of slightly cooking vegetables before you preserve them. The process remains the same for all vegetables, although the time of blanching varies with each one. First, put on a pot of water to boil while preparing the rest of the steps. Fill a large bowl half full with cool water and add ice. Use a large pot or bowl that will hold a colander. Both the ice water bath and the pot with colander should be close to the boiling water. Use slotted spoons or tongs (depends on the vegetable) for moving the vegetables from boiling water to ice water to holding spot. Prepare the vegetables by washing and cutting into the size portion you want to preserve. Have enough freezer bags or freezer containers ready to use. It's a good idea to label prior to starting the blanching process. Put the name of vegetable and date frozen on the label.

Place the vegetables in the boiling water. Only put enough vegetables in pot that you can easily remove in a short amount of time. Follow blanching time from below or from another source.

At the end of the blanching time (most vegetables will be from one to three minutes), remove the vegetables from boiling water and immediately submerge in ice water bath for the same amount of time you used in the blanching process.

At end of ice water time, remove vegetables and place in colander to drain before placing in freezer bag or container.

Start the process all over again, if you have more vegetables. If you do more than a couple of batches, you'll need to replace ice in ice water bath.

The point of the whole process is to partially cook while retaining the best flavors (and color) of the vegetable. When you thaw to use, cut down cooking time by the approximate time you used for blanching.

Here are the blanching times for vegetables I've blanched and then frozen:

Cabbage – cut into wedges or shred. Wedges – 3 minutes. Shredded – 1 ½ minutes

Corn – husk and remove silk – 5-6 minutes; then remove from ice water bath and cut kernels from the cob

Green beans – ends removed and broken into 1-inch pieces – 3 minutes

Peas – removed from the pod – 2 minutes

Zucchini – shredded – 2-3 minutes

Garlic Braids

What to do when the garlic crop finally produces? Braid them, of course!

We'd been trying to grow garlic for several years, but Robert just hadn't discovered the proper conditions or timing for them. These he put in the ground in North Carolina in the fall. By the time we returned in May, they were ready to be harvested.

They can be stored for six months or so under the proper conditions, but we still had far too many for our own usage, and I wasn't sure where I had room to store them with the proper dryness and air required. Then I remembered something I've always been tempted to buy but the cost was always too prohibitive. The garlic braid is an attractive and great way to keep the garlic for months. Plus, I had enough garlic to make braids for my daughter and a couple of friends.

Here's how we did it.

Harvest garlic with leaves intact. Lay them in a cool and dry place—we used our porch and placed them on newspaper. After approximately two weeks, the green on the leaves begins to brown. Robert chose the bulbs with the biggest bulbs for planting in the fall. The rest I prepared for braiding.

Clean the bulbs. Remove any lingering dirt before you braid it. In some cases, you may be able to remove the dirt and other residue by brushing it away with your fingers. I used both my fingers and a slightly damp cloth. On some of the bulbs, I removed several layers of outer dry skin to get rid of dirt. Do not remove all the outer layers.

Trim the garlic. There are usually long, scraggly roots attached to the bottom bulbs, so cut those to approximately ¼-inch. Also trim away any of the leaves that are scraggly looking.

Soak the garlic stems. You want the bulbs' leaves to be pliable so they're easier to braid. There are two ways to do this, but most importantly, do not get the bulbs wet during this process. You only want the leaves damp enough to be flexible. You can wrap the leaves in wet towels and leave for 20-30 minutes or longer. I tried this the first year, and it didn't seem to get them pliable enough. The second year, I used a different method, which I liked much better. Fill a bowl or sink with lukewarm water and soak the garlic so just the leaves are submerged. Soak for 15-30 minutes until they are flexible.

Select three largest bulbs and crisscross them. It is suggested that for the best braids, you use twelve bulbs. I've used less than that to good effect. As you're sorting the ones that you'll use, set aside the three largest bulbs to serve as the start of the braid. Lay them on a flat surface with one bulb in the center, one to its left, and one to its right. The center bulb's leaves should be pointed at you, while the other two leaves are crisscrossed over one another to form an X over the center bulb. It helps to secure the place where the bulbs overlap with a piece of twine. Make sure that the piece of twine you use is long enough to knot over the bulbs with enough excess that you can secure additional bulbs that you place in the braid.

Start adding bulbs. Place a fourth bulb over the existing bundle, so it matches up with the center bulb. Use the excess twine to secure the fourth bulb to the stack to make it easier when you start to braid. Next, take two more bulbs and align them with the two diagonal bulbs in a crisscross fashion.

Begin braiding. With all of the bulbs' leaves lined up, it's time to start the braid. Make sure that you're grabbing the two sets of leaves for each section as you begin braiding. Take the two leaves from the right side and cross them under the middle leaves, so they become the centerpieces. Next, take the two leaves on the left and cross them under the middle leaves. Repeat using twine to secure as needed. I only used twine on the fourth bulb and then at the end.

Add more bulbs. Once you've started the braid, you can add three bulbs. You should line the leaves up with the existing ends of the braids as you did with the second set, so one aligns with the left section, one aligns with the center, and one aligns with the right. Start braiding again for one or two passes and repeat the process until you've added all of your bulbs. I've used as few as six bulbs so I could give braids as gifts.

Finish braiding and secure the entire garlic braid. After you've added all of the garlic, you should continue braiding the leaves until you get to the end. Use another piece of twine to tie off the end and secure the entire braid. I then used the twine to help me hang the bulbs.

Note: The first year I braided garlic, my husband only had green twine. I used it but it was very conspicuous in the braids. The next year I made sure I had brown which blends in better with the leaves.

THE CYCLE BEGINS ALL OVER AGAIN

GARDENING, EVEN in the north, is a year-round process. In Florida, the summer serves as the time to plan and rest before the fall planting season begins. In the north that time occurs in December and January.

With a big enough garden, each season can provide food in different stages.

The hard work under the blazing summer sun is forgotten as soon as the fresh vegetables hit our palates. Gardening provides us with sustenance for our health, but it also provides a lifeline for our soul.

THE END

REFERENCES

Ball Blue Book Guide to Preserving – This is the most valuable of all the books in my preserving library. Not only does it go over the basics of canning, it offers some great recipes for the bounty.

The Big Book of Preserving the Harvest – 150 Recipes for Freezing, Canning, Drying, and Picking Fruits and Vegetables by Carol W. Costenbader – Another good source for technique and recipes.

Everything Canning & Preserving Book – All you need to know to enjoy natural, healthy foods year round – By Patricia Telesco with Jeanne P. Maack – I don't use this book very much, but I'd recommend to anyone just starting out in the world of preserving your produce.

Home-Canning and Preserving – by Anne Borella – I'm not sure if this book is still in print, but if it is, it's a great basic book on canning published in 1974.

Animal, Vegetable, Miracle – by Barbara Kingsolver – A comprehensive book about one family's attempt to eat only local food for an entire year. The book also presents compelling reasons to garden.

Llewellyn's 2013 Moon Sign Book – Robert uses this book to find out the best time for starting seeds and planting seedlings.

Here are a few sites we've consulted over the years:
   http://www.organicgardening.com
   http://www.howtocompost.org
   http://www.composting101.com

WORKS BY P.C. ZICK

Behind the Love Romances

Behind the Altar Book One - All seems perfect in Leah's life until tattoo artist Dean rides his Harley into her heart in this story of forbidden love.

Behind the Bar Book Two – Reggie and Susie almost lose each other as they struggle to overcome the past.

Behind the Curtain Book Three – Lisa returns to Victory with a reality TV crew, and Tommy and she struggle to remain friends despite a growing attraction. The whole town is turned upside down as television cameras attempt to capture it all.

Behind the Door Book Four – Sally Jean as she struggles to find true love even though she believes she doesn't deserve it. Dr. Brett helps her discover her true inner beauty.

Rivals in Love Series –Follow the Crandall family siblings as they find love and navigate careers.

Love on Trial – Oldest Crandall sibling, Jude, is on opposite sides of the courtroom with Malik, a slick lawyer with an Iranian mother who pushes to bring Jude and Malik together. She's helped by Sofia Mancini Crandall, Jude's mother. But it's two dogs that fall in love first and show Jude and Malik that love crosses all boundaries.

Love on Board –Rock Crandall is a pilot who is surprised by his new female co-pilot. He must change his view of the world as Sabrina shows him a whole different side to life than what he's known.

Love on Track – Race car driver Stone spends his life on the track with precision like focus. It's never left time for romance until his childhood friend who happens to be Jude's best friend forces him to step out of the driver's seat for a different kind of ride.

Love on Air– Diamond or "Mond" Crandall stars in this story about a rising star on a cable news show. When Hope Colson shows up on his show, their on-screen presence sizzles while off-screen it simmers with unease.

Love on Course – The youngest sibling, Turq, works as a chef in one of Chicago's finest restaurants, but he's tired and lonely after his girlfriend Cindy moves away. Trips to Italy and Ireland and questions from Cindy bring him to decisions about his priorities.

Love on Stage – Ruby, the only other female Crandall sibling, seeks stardom in Hollywood, but is drawn home for a family crisis and ends up finding a love that might change the course of her career.

Love on Holiday – Celebrate the fortieth wedding anniversary of the couple who started the whole thing. Nolan and Sofia face some struggles as the rest of the family plans a surprise anniversary celebration for Christmas Eve.

Florida Fiction Series

Tortoise Stew – Politics, murder, and chaos in rural Florida reign supreme in a story where love triumphs over it all.

Trails in the Sand – Family secrets, an oil spill, and redemption create a roller coaster ride for journalist Caroline Carlisle.

Native Lands- A novel rich in intrigue and history as a tribe of Native Americans, thought to be extinct, fight to save their beloved heritage.

Smoky Mountain Sweet Romances

Minty's Kiss - a sweet Christmas novella set in the foothills of the Smoky Mountains in Murphy, North Carolina. Two childhood sweethearts, one lonely little girl, and a smart kitty hope to find happiness as Christmas approaches.

Misty Mountain – The characters from *Minty's Kiss* return as Lacy and George struggle to overcome the heartbreaks from their previous relationships.

Mountain Miracles – David and Cecelia—two new folks and strangers to one another—come to Murphy to start businesses. He wants to reconnect to his past and she wants to forget hers, which brings them on a collision course to love.

A Merry Mountain Christmas – Fran, the mother to everyone, finds herself alone and wondering how she can make a difference. When her first love returns to town, he brings more than romance to her life.

Smoky Mountain Romances – All four Smoky Mountain Romances in one book!

Montauk Romances

Love on the Wind, A Montauk Romance, Book One - Six years of traveling for her television series has left host Kiley Nelson longing for a place to call her own. Spending a weekend at her girlfriend's beach house is the perfect reprieve, especially when she purchases property to finally settle down. But her peaceful escape is shaken when she smashes into a car containing the sinfully sexy and infuriated passenger, Jeff Hammond, who immediately melts her heart.

Jingle Bell Love, A Montauk Romance, Book Two - Denny and Jill find themselves lustfully drawn to one another. When friends disapprove, they hatch a pact to be friends with secret benefits. This steamy romance jingles all the bells for the Christmas season.

Other Works of Fiction

Live from the Road (A Magical Route 66 Novel) – The reader heads out on an often humorous, yet harrowing, journey as Meg Newton and Sally Sutton seek a change in the mundane routine of their lives. Joined by their daughters, they set off on a journey of salvation enhanced by the glories of the Mother Road.

A Lethal Legacy (Psychological Suspense) - A fascinating study of human expectations, failings, and redemption filled with lust and forbidden lovers.

Third Base - When Adriana Moretti meets baseball star Tomas Vegas, she's surprised by his kindness. While Tomas puts all his energy into winning the World Series for the Pittsburgh Pirates, he's thrown off his game by the brilliant and beautiful Adriana, who owns a multi-million-dollar business she started with her late husband.

Nonfiction

Eclectic Leanings - Musings from a Writer's Soul: Essays, Creative Nonfiction, and Short Stories - Award-winning author P.C. Zick offers up a collection of her writings, which span the course of more than two decades. The collection contains her columns, blog posts, editorials, creative nonfiction, and short stories.

From Seed to Table - Gardening techniques, organic gardening, canning vegetables, and recipes galore.

Odyssey to Myself (Essays nonfiction) – The people of Morocco, Italy, Panama, and Chile come to life through the experiences of the author as she absorbs the cultures so different from her own.

Civil War Journal of a Union Soldier (Memoir nonfiction) – My great grandfather's journal from his days as a soldier. It's a personal account of war and all its sundry causes and effects from the eyes of a man who fought it.

Civil War Journal from the 2nd Michigan – An expanded version of Civil War Journal of a Union Soldier, this book contains the complete journal of Harmon Camburn (1842-1906) as well as more local history about Lenawee County in southeastern Michigan and the great abolitionist, Laura S. Haviland, who was related through marriage to Harmon Camburn. Further annotations of the journal and the additional appendixes provide a portrait of both time and place.

The Author's Journey: A Road Map for Writers – From Draft to Published Book – A reference book to take the mystery out of writing and publishing a book, whether through traditional channels or as an Indie Author. And if your questions aren't answered, Zick provides a lengthy bibliography for all aspects of writing, editing, publishing, and promoting your book.

ABOUT P.C. ZICK

Bestselling author P.C. Zick describes herself as a storyteller no matter what she writes. And she writes in a variety of genres, including romance, contemporary fiction, and creative nonfiction. She's won various awards for her essays, columns, editorials, articles, and novels.

The three novels in her **Florida Fiction Series** contain stories of Florida and its people and environment, which she credits as giving her a rich base for her storytelling. She says, "Florida's quirky and abundant wildlife—both human and animal—supply my fiction with tales almost too weird to be believable."

P.C. writes both sweet and steamy romances. The sweet contemporary romances in her **Smoky Mountain Romances,** are set in southwest North Carolina. Another sweet romance series, **Rivals in Love,** contains seven stories about finding and keeping love alive. The novels follow the Crandall family of Chicago as the siblings find love despite their focus on successful careers.

Her steamy romances go from Florida to Long Island. The **Behind the Love** series, set in a small fictional town in Florida, feature a community of people who form bonds as they learn to overcome the challenges of their youth. Her **Montauk Romances** are set in and around Long Island and feature simple, yet sophisticated beach houses designed with romance in mind. The two books in this set are filled with steamy scenes as love grows and thrives.

Zick offers a variety of nonfiction books, which include a book on vegetable gardening, a compilation of her essays and short stories from her decades-long career as a writer, and a primer for writers on taking an idea and turning it into a published book. She has also published and annotated the journal of her great-grandfather based on his experiences as a Union soldier during the Civil War.

Her novels contain elements of romance with strong female characters, handsome heroes, and descriptive settings. And all of her works express her philosophy of living lightly upon this earth with love, laughter, and passion.

She and her husband split their time between Tallahassee, Florida, and the Smoky Mountains where they enjoy gardening, kayaking, and hiking.

You can keep track of P.C. Zick's new releases and special promotions by visiting her website, www.pczick.com.